WERE YOU ALWAYS A CRIMINAL?

FREDDIE GREENFIELD

Fag Rag Books Boston, 1989

Special thanks to George Dimsey for editing and helping make most of the selections for this book and no less appreciative thanks to Fag Rag staff, Charley Shively, Siong Huat Chua and Mike Riegle for the nitty gritty aspect, typesetting, layout, proofreading and of course their sharply attuned collective ear to my particular sound. Added thanks to Bruce McLay for technical assistance. Siong Huat and Chris Pomiecko formatted and laid out the pages.

Mug shot on back cover and cover design by Chris Pomiecko

Fag Rag Books
Box 331 Kenmore Station
Boston MA 02215

TABLE OF CONTENTS

INTRODUCTION

WARNING: READING THIS BOOK MAY BE HAZARDOUS

A doctor authority once introduced juicy picture-story books-films. Like a lawyer, the white coat explained that the work you are about to begin has socially redeeming value (if only as a specimen of pathology).

In this context *Were You Always A Criminal* is unreservedly anti-social, anti-society. Family and social pretentions flushed down the toilet. No new society. No anti-society pushed. Another world society's just there. In "Orangeburge to Macon and So Forth:" "Planed to Boston then by automobile to Miami Beach on the nod. Sexual liaisons with prescription writing physicians one passenger in automobile that's what the passengers job was making croakers."

Redeeming? Not ecological like returning glass bottles. Nor Christian, nor anti-Christian. Jewish? Beyond Good and Evil? "Beyond Hebraic ABC's:" "Lonely fruitless attempts with my cock to simulate a foreskin, try as I might. Only a year away from entering manhood, my parents inferred, and you remain totally ignorant of the hebraic ritual performance, 'What are we paying to send you to hebrew school for if you're not learning anything?' was the wailing lament I'd hear regularly. Secretly I was learning, from an older man, an ex-cop, how to control my sphincter."

Value? For only $7.95 *Were You Always A Criminal* is a steal, a bargain. Buy several— for gifts, stocking stuffers, crotch fillers, beach reading. They'll love you for the thought, the size of the gift.

Freddie describes socially redeeming value in his approach (or flight from) pulp romance in "Meanwhile:" "I'd met Ricky in New York City, Bryant Park, the park behind the Fifth Avenue Public Library.... it slopped out of me husky voiced, me telling him how

v

much I cared for him. Tell me you love me. Tell me you love me. Like I've said already it was Ricky's often most repeated line. You mean a lot to me. You mean an awful lot to me I told him oh I don't know how many times."

"Both Dead and Buried" includes Ma, Pa and Ricky (Miss Hush): "It's only now with them both dead and buried that I have a clear picture of their insanity and their willingness to infect their children with that very same insanity infect their children by association. So anyways Hush sat on the curbstone downstairs and my mother pipes up with he's crying he's weeping and he's saying between sobs he won't leave until you talk to him. Don't interfere ma don't interfere.... Get off my ear ma get off my ear is what I wanted to tell my mother what does she know what does she know what it's all about how me and Hush we'd suck cocks and assholes in public toilets stealing wallets out of different men's pockets while they had their trousers unspecting down around their ankles."

I first met Miss Hush (Ricky) in 1965 but didn't meet Freddie until 1973 reading in Stone Soup Storefront Gallery. Going on and on about subway men's rooms, blowing & shooting up, IRT "A" train, station by station; none of the straight boys seemed offended because they weren't listening, waiting to read themselves, waiting to become stars. Sal Farinella, David Emerson Smith, myself, we heard the music right away...

Freddie comes and goes in the sea: Mystic River Harbor, Revere Beach; Jones Beach; Coney Island; North Beach; Key West; L Street Beach. A Harvard historian wrote about the "unmitigated ugliness of Chelsea;" and was glad for the Mystic Bridge connecting Beacon Hill with the North Shore without descending into the depths. Not Portnoy's complaint but Jews who eked out pittances beside the Mystic River & along the Revere Beach Boulevard midway & boxing...

Toni said Oh do you know Freddie; yes I said he's a writer; the best Toni agreed; his prescriptions always passed. Better forgeries than the fabulous war on drugs. For example: acetylsalicylic acid; either doctors are stupid or they lie if they say the pain reliever they'd want most on a deserted island would be acetylsalicylic acid (med students, the correct answer is not ibuprophen).

He can be sly & canny; a bottle of paragoric and two puppies licking his toes begging, o please daddy give me a bottle before I go to bed; o no not now, sit, sit, roll over; do you really need it? well ok but dont keep nagging...

What's Freddie poetry and what's Freddie prose? Who can say; just thumb through the scorched records of old *Fag Rags* or scan *Amusement Business* (Boston: Good Gay Poets, 1976). One printer rejected *Amusement Business* because Bibles ran over their presses & we got even at Boston's Gay Pride Rally in 1977 by burning a King James Bible inside a metal wok; Freddie & I experimented with various inflammables before we went on stage; he held the wok while I threw in the holy texts; next time we'll have pot holders— too hot to carry...

Or Freddie with esophagus cancer in intensive care not being able to answer; the oscillator traced the strain of not being able to speak. A fellow patient with terminal pancreas cancer; Lee Stone & I gross the wife & son who were getting on the dying man's nerves; they call the nurse; he smiles as he follows, saying good luck with his eyes. Freddie recovers fully except for a few millimeters of esophogus which go down the drain...

& his family tried to disinherit him. Were You Always a Criminal? they ask & we got some of their money & we're using it to publish *Were You Always a Criminal?* If that's not revenge, what is? Justice? Have we proved that the Criminal Justice system really works? Certainly not until his unpublished magnum opus *Money Honey* finds a printer & publisher.

"Work" & "Word" &c aren't words to throw around lightly. George Dimsey (who knows the insides of this book like the guts of a fish) says we're lucky to find out about Mickey Finn and The Jockey, Max, Tony, Greg, Steve, Roy, Bobby, John, the Polish policeman, Jimmy Tyler and so forth. But we have yet to hear about Big Al, Andy the Midget, Joe the Bug or Jacky the Kook.

"Grind Store Agent with a Captial 'F'" left me wondering just what is a "grind store." In carnival midways, so Freddie says, a grind store's tops, the elite amusement business hustlers run them. They're best grinding dollars out of marks (marks are us dear readers). Freddie runs a grand Grind Store in *Were You Always a Criminal?* Strictly professional, jockey, boxer, cocksucker, junkie, rabbi, cop, doctor. Strictly professional, you understand? We're talking about the amusement business, everyone's a winner, step right up, test your skills. Productivity defeated easily. *Were You Always a Criminal?* comes out just in time for Freddie's sixtieth birthday. Keep on playing to win, one more throw'll do it....

Charley Shively

L istening to myself again after all these years have gone by it's still the same record played over and over again the same bluesy number.....

Williams Junior High School, 1943
(Freddie kneeling second from right)

1 Beyond Hebraic ABC's

T oltz, homeroom, music teacher. Dineen, manual training. Kepnes, mathematics. Glickstien for science and Brodbine for seventh grade english. I took another language, french I, but forget the teachers name (was it Delaney, Miss, may I be excused? I have to go to the basement and take a). Mr Wright was the principal of Williams Junior High School and all the pupils feared his thick wooden ruler.

Did you ever? Me? No. Ever feel the pain of Wrights ruler across your palm? Nay.

In the afternoon at 3 oclock it was to hebrew school and Mister Cushmans class. Baking unyeasted bread on their bare heads the tribes of israel walked across the parted red sea. Chasing the israelites close behind came the philistines, but, lo and behold, as the last israelite safely reached the other side, the red sea swallowed the philistines.

The jew killers, uncircumsized, were my playmates, my love objects. The sliding members head revealing the mysterious skin beneath my academic efforts.

At twelve years of age my sexual inclinations were overpowering and those inclinations saw me chosen for every school

3

athletic team. In class spent day dreaming of sex and sports. Sports and sex took over my psyche completely. Lonely fruitless attempts with my cock to simulate a foreskin, try as I might. Only a year away from entering manhood, my parents inferred, and you remain totally ignorant of the hebraic ritual performance, "What are we paying to send you to hebrew school for if you're not learning anything?" was the wailing lament I'd hear regularly. Secretly I was learning, from an older man, an ex-cop, how to control my sphincter. For fifty cents a lesson it was decided to send me to a private tutor, a rabbi, who would teach me my obligatory religious instructions. Rabbi Kepnes, the mathematic instructors bearded orthodox pater. As far as the American grammar school went, that was a secondary issue.

"You need a spanking," said Rabbi Kepnes, in gutteral english, "help make you learn better, understand?"

Yes, I understood. It was common knowledge among my playmates, students of Rabbi Kepnes, how spankings went with the lessons. A light spanking with a cat o' ninetails over the rabbis lap with ones bare ass exposed. I knew the scene, as intuitive and so very sexually inclined in an exciting and exploratory way, at twelve years of age. Far back as I can remember there were no taboos for me when it came to lusting for the touch of the human physical form.

Born June 20th 1929, a child victim of the economic depression, I was learning rapidly how adults coveted a youthful body. My ex-cop gratefully shelling a dollar bill daily to me after we'd consummate our bedroom escapades. I never asked for money directly and would have given out regardless as sex in itself for me was reward enough, but, I suppose it was a way, as far as the mentality of the ex-cop went, of keeping me on the leash, so to speak.

Fifty cents a day for lessons given to me by my parents to be

4

given to Rabbi Kepnes, Kepnes the elder scholar of talmudic law.

With the rabbis finger pointing at the first letter of the hebraic abc's we'd start our lessons, "pronounce aleph."

"Arleph"

"No. no. Aleph, aleph."

"Aleleph?" This would go on for ten or fifteen minutes then out would come the rabbis cat o ninetails. "Do you want me to take off my pants, rabbi?" I'd remove my trousers and closely watch the rabbis demeanor change, at the sight of my bare boy ass, from one of a didacticists frustration with a pupil to a fervent state of erotic ecstacy. Over rabbis lap for five or ten lashes with the rabbinical teachers leather thongs. The spanking never administered severe enough to register complaints to one's parents, payee's of my religious training.

In 1941, for me at least, 50¢ was a lot of money. Rabbi Kepnes and the hebrew lessons bored me to distraction. Quite a few times I'd skip a lesson and pocket the 50¢. Trouble was, though, my favorite street playing area was close by Rabbi Kepnes's storefront classroom. If two days in succession went by without me showing for my hebrew instructions there would be rabbi peeking through the above clear glass of the storefront classroom windows. Bottom half covered with a diamond shaped patterned paper to help keep jew killer (gentile) eyes at bay, no doubt. Across from rabbi Kepnes's, also, there were a couple of abandoned tenements, where on many occasions, feeling flush with rabbis 50¢ in my pocket, I'd take Eddie, a young potential polish jew killer, and, with a nickel or dime enticement, suck Eddie's uncircumcised thing ending usually by sticking my own thing between the young polacks smooth hairless thighs and with the help of spit simulate a fuck.

Everything physical about the rabbi I found unattractive. A sour smell of decay that comes from people who rarely remove their outer clothing. The intrigue about the spanking scene with rabbi Kepnes was that it gave me control of an adult authoritarian figure. Show you the control I had; wasn't long before it was me doing the spanking with rabbi lying face down on a studio couch covered with my rabbis silk-lined long caftan coat, bare-assed naked, feigning pain with each thwack I gave my rabbi, "Oo, aah, oh, oo," my talmudic scholar would moan rapidly jiggling that nude rabbinical rear end until climax on the black silk would result. Stains on the inside of a caftan coat don't come from snot. Soon as my daily hebrew lessons grew tedious I'd tell rabbi Kepnes, "You've been bad rabbi. Pull your pants down, rabbi. Come, lay down on the bed, rabbi, I'm going to give you a spanking." It went without saying that the lesson money was not expected. Sort of worked like an exchange of spankings. First me, so's rabbi Kepnes could become aroused by seeing my young boyass, then rabbis turn. (Today I only regret not being more sadistic and really lashing the rabbis ass a lot harder so that my imprint would have left a few scarred welts.)

Anyway, a year of the bit with the rabbi and my confirmation day at a synogogue took place. I struggled through the ritual recitation with a barely audible mumble. Finished with a sigh of relief as family well wishers shook my hand exclaiming loudly, "Congratualtions, today you are a man." Rabbi Kepnes beside me voicing the yiddish counter part, "A mench, a mensch." Me, quietly wanting to say, "Drop your baggy trousers rabbi and show the congregation the ass that made my confirmation as a mensch possible."

No if ands and buts, jewish boys must be bah mitsvahd; must get their ass licked. Must observe the rules of male authority. The rabbis ass was an open invitation for rebellion.

What'd it look like, your rabbis ass? A full, firm, round apple-cheeked type with a gray-greenish-yellow complexion. A clean underweared 'fruit of the loom' fellow, my rabii Kepnes. Although I dimly recall on cold days my rabbi wore long johns, kind that have a shit split opening so when I beat the rabbi in sub-zero weather rabbi would accomodate me by hunching up the ass and with both hands reach behind stretching the cloth shit split opening for better exposure.

Jewboy, so far removed, was I, from a jewboy culture. My culture was the faggothood culture, only I didn't know it, I wasn't aware of it at the time the ultimate social forces had me preparing "for your bar mitsvah," they did say, "the most important event in your life, boy." I had my own physical self to satisfy, yet. Yet nobody ever told me that. At twelve years of age I felt the catholics were my immediate superiors because they had uncircumcised cocks. (In those days circumcision wasn't such a formal practice in christian and non-sectarian hospitals as it is today.)

The yiddish fag is well hidden. The orthodox rabbi is covered by so much clothing as to appear sexually invulnerable. For me seeing my rabbis bare ass could be likened to a non-erotic burlesque strip tease. I was twelve years old having two full-time affairs. One with a ten year old male polack whose rectum, my goal in life at that particular juncture in time, was to penetrate with my cut hebrew cock; I'd already managed to get my tongue up there. The other one with a fifty-year-old irish ex-cop whose rather large foreskinned prick, fortunately, I daily guided up my vaselined hole. Anyway, scenes with my rabbi were extra curricular and had a tendency to bore me so preoccupied was I anticipating getting naked to suck and fuck with my two catholic goyisha shacoorum (gentile bums). It was a shame, true, here I was a year away from being officially declared a man and I hadn't had any sex play with a jew yet. I suppose there were othere jewboys who liked doing the sexual things I did, but in the ghetto where I was raised I never

7

found one, and I'll add it wasn't for want of trying. I pried, I poked and I rubbed many a jew cock as a youth and all I ever got was a flushed red blush in return. As it's said, to make a long story short, by the time I bumped into the rabbis bare ass gyrations on a caftan coat I was completely turned off by jew pricks and behinds. (I was very fond of stuffed kishkee it so resembled my ex-cop's cock. Made to resemble a huge sausage, a cows intestine filled with flour and seasoning and sewed at both ends then baked or roasted in a hot oven.)

2 Save a Good Boy! Save a Good Boy!

Way it's remembered, lips, turning purple. Shoot salt, table salt out of the shaker on Pearl Street the cities last commercial hotel. Way it's heard at the arena gamblers yelling trying to influence the referee, stop it. Save a good boy! Save a good boy!

He's asthmatic. He's got bottles of adrenalin. Has me laughing today. I'd walked into the room while his chest was heaving and his lips were starting to appear bloodless, his face a clayish gray. Rub ice on him one of us said. Where? Where should we rub the ice? Between his legs, between his legs. Between his legs no apparent life. Call the police. Let me say that was all I had to hear, call the police.

Took off from coast to coast and back settling down selling the automobile for junk. Substantial in size the lifeless hunk between his legs the one with chest heaving rapidly massaging the area that had been circumsized. Now living for a short while in flop houses charging twenty cents a night clean sheet and small towel. Elevated had not been removed rattling by getting used to sound from speed highs frantic with sexual urges unrefined.

Lacked a business hustle. Remembered the one with heaving chest graduated bass player embezzled front desk clerk. As I've said that's all I had to hear, call the police. Drove night and day cashing phony prescriptions before meeting a lover buck teeth

9

tall six foot legs wrapped about his waist thick foreskin busing tables in cafeteria. Got me a job until looking in mirror the reflection becoming awry. Laughing on account of all that needed to be done was to have filled a syringe, filled it with adrenalin. Anyways he lived and a slue of arrests were the end results avoided in my secondhand automobile an eight cylinder Buick two new tires until brakes ceased to exist planning complete stops hundreds of feet from desired spots pumping and snapping my sphincter.

Rifling bags for narcotics country club door concession dinner dances and other catered affairs in the kitchen snacks of chopped liver on crackers spreads of mayonnaised egg salad. In health exercise section is where the shit was taken, downstairs. Must do something about people from the town coming into parking lot and stealing hubcaps the boss said. Call the police, that's all I had to hear.

At the boxing matches, ringside. Ringside at the boxing matches later after fights fuck in bed toilet paper the wiping ass after.

And it's where I first heard it. Ringside, at the boxing matches. I was twelve years old. Jim, first person ever to fuck me, went with him to initial boxing matches. We went to his bed after the fights were over and fucked when he took it out or rather when it slid out of its own accord I went into Jim's bathroom and wiped my ass with his toilet paper. Save a good boy! Save a good boy!

===

3 Forget About Mickey Finn and The Jockey

Mickey Finn and The Jockey? They were familiar names. Mickey I knew casually meeting him for the first time the night Marty Zide tied his clothing in bed sheets and threw it out of a sixth floor hall window into the narrow alley like sidestreet below where I sat behind the wheel of Marty Zide's rental car. It was out the window of The Touraine, Hotel Touraine. Finn had quit using stuff but me and Marty had this shit load of half grain morphine tablets. The majority of the people Mickey Finn knew thought he had gone off the deep end giving up stuff standing on his head doing yoga exercises. It was odd because his friends, ones we knew, hustled... boosters, racetrack touts and so forth. Anyways, here was Mickey Finn watching for me and Marty at three in the morning making sure when we picked up Marty's bundle that no suspicious cops were in sight. It was offered to him, morphine, he refused. Marty turned his face away from Mickey and smirked, so did I.

Jockey Martin. That was The Jockey's last name, Martin. He wasn't riding at the track, getting any mounts, because in the latter few years he'd been in and out of trouble with the law, everybody knows how moral state racing commissions are. Those jockeys, individuals who've been around the jockeys dressing rooms at various horse tracks have said, those jockeys have some of the biggest pricks they'd ever seen. It's also said they have small hands, dainty almost, but wrists that are powerful. They need it, strong wrists, one hand flailing the rump of their mounts

11

with a whip while the other hand grips the reins. A race riders grip, probably they hold the reins loose like someone does to control a pool cue, firm but loose. So, anyways as far as The Jockey goes, he's one of the ones I'd never actually met in the flesh.

Suddenly, say if I wanted to find out, all of a sudden what'd The Jockey's cock look like? Who could I go to? Who could I ask? Mickey Finn? Marty? Marty Zide's another story. I'd spent some time with Marty Zide and I knew he had a fat hunk between his legs. But what good was it when he only thought about gambling and drugs. He thought of himself as an A-one handicapper pointing out to me, see this it ran a mile in so many minutes and so many seconds. Yes, it wanted to make me cry almost, what good is your fat prick to me, Marty Zide, when you smell of drug sickness. When's the last time it was hard Marty Zide? Anyway, so that same morning we said goodby to Mickey Finn and with someone else Marty Zide had hanging around him we left in Marty's rental car for Atlantic City. Marty had got the shit load of morphine tablets, the half grain tablets, from a couple of really aggressive people. They weren't drug addicts. Plus not being drug addicts themselves they had a grossly exaggerated idea about the stuffs actual worth. Alright, so the Atlantic City trip was an evasive action on Marty Zides part. Of course I was in for some of the drugs because I was providing some of the money for the trip with my hustling a short change scam and in the process teaching Zide to do it himself. Actually the person that Marty took with us he'd met in a poolroom. An attractive fair skinned irish guy but an uptight sexless snob that you know once we arrived in Atlantic City and checked into a motel he never removed his clothes. Then too he was a prude that didn't use stuff which in a way was alright with me and Martin Zide. I mean that was all the more for us.

I don't know. Anyway it was there in Atlantic City that Marty Zide pulled this unforgivable shit on me. Suddenly he gets overly protective or possessive about his shit load of morphine doling me out a small portion with the excuse the reason he's

Jockey in Winners Circle at Hialeah

cutting me down is that he has to sell the stuff and give the money to the couple he got the stuff from originally, the two aggressive people I've mentioned. Well that's a crock of shit I told him. Finally, anyway I fell asleep and in the morning when I woke Marty Zide and the irish guy were gone. A good thing I had hid some morphine and most of the money I had on me. Funny part is I wasn't angry. I had morphine. I had money didn't I and didn't it look like I'd never actually get to relate to Martin Zide and his big fat prick that never gets hard?

What did I do? I took my suitcase down to the Atlantic City bus station checked it into one of those twentyfive cent lockers and headed for the toilet hoping to discover a stall with a glory hole. That's just what happened and I had a few breaking the monotony.

The confrontation? Yes, so anyways I had a few hours before a bus would leave Atlantic City. Alright I decided to take a walk on the boardwalk. I'm walking along the boardwalk and who should I spot in one of those bicycle rickshaws, Marty Zide and the irish guy. I just stopped them the blood literally drained from Marty Zides face. Talk about guilt. And he didn't even know I had the cache of morphine tablets I had hid. Anyways, I gave him a verbal blasting. When getting to the point of asking him how could he leave me in such a mess with no stuff, very little money and so forth and what did he now propose to do to rectify matters? Anyways, as I held him hostage, so to speak, him and the irish guy debarked the rickshaw, he sent the irish quy to a hotel room they had booked to get his shit load of morphine tablets so as to make a settlement with me.

To make a long story short don't think I didn't take advantage of his personal guilt, yet. Yet, had Martin Zide been suddenly, say all of a sudden sexually free with me in regards to his big fat prick by attempting a get together and with me trying to produce a hardon I probably would have not been as demanding as I was when it came to the stuff and everything. I mean forget about Mickey Finn and The Jockey.

14

4   ... A Sadly Mistaken Lie

T he minute he said to me if he'd had his way he'd get rid of the pushers this is supposed to be on account of me on account of I was using dope. You know what I mean? as though I was out of it completely, didn't have a choice. Is it true when you use hard stuff your desire for sex is gone? No, that's a sadly mistaken lie. A lie lots of times gay drinkers spout, sneering, "oh, don't fool with him he's a drug addict." Types I've been home with fall asleep before anything happens smelling like a brewery. So, when he said that about the dealers I bought my stuff from I had to make this move reeevaluating my friendship with this quean I sometimes traveled with, and worked for, once in awhile.

About the dope and his awful statement it took place in NYC. He had a couple of concessions with The Paul Miller Show playing on parking lots of shopping centers around Westchester County. I had a habit then but despite junk I managed to suck a good few cocks on a day to day basis.

How it came about I had him with me when I went to buy my dope? Anyway, I do know he insisted he wanted to come and I certainly made no secret how enamoured I was with especially heroin; speed, too, on occasion. He likes young dark puerto ricans with big cocks jostling around loose in their pants (it was a hot summer and the trousers most kids wore were thin). I left him on a busy corner as I crossed the street to get my dope. When I got back I wanted to get rid of him and go shoot my dope; after, if I was into it I'd visit a few subway toilets (keep my sexual sissiness alive). Before I'd got back he'd connected with a boy just like I've described so now there was no problem for me to get rid of him or if worse had come to worse? Couldn't have him actually watch me shoot the stuff such a knocker as he was for dope. Good, he was off with his big pricked puerto rican boy. He really loved giving those kids $20 bills, these ones who lacked the finesse to ask for a fiver (this wasn't 42nd street - it wasn't the eastside - it was uptown broadway in the 90s).

I'd love to have been relating on a sexual level - purely on a sexual level - but you know I had to get up and start each day with an injection. How many people not directly involved with hard dope understand? Who's supposed to educate them? Not only a sadly mistaken lie but a vicious lie as well is perpetrated about the general behavior of drug addicted queans.

The whole thing was everyday you have to make a meet for stuff cautiously so as not to be observed by police, and the police, they are everywhere. So, alright, what I'm saying is a lot of spent energy is used. Money? Money's nothing if the goods are decent. With that and still able daily to get an allotment of cock a quean no matter how dissipated he looks has a reason to be proud.

---

5 Dickie's Word Against Anybody's

One thing about being jewish in NYC even though I'm originally from Boston is that there were a lot of other jewish dope fiends nearer my age. Dickie for instance. Dickie Wynofsky and plus he was supposed to be gay like I was, only more people, jewish dope fiends, knew about Dickie than knew about me. He'd brag how Gersh punched him around, giggling even how he had all these black and blue marks that Gersh gave him. I think they did a bit together on Hart's Island where the cemetery is.

Me and Dickie Wynofsky did a drug cure together. I mean that's what it's supposed to be, a drug cure, where they take you down gradually. That's where and when he told me how Gersh would punch him around. It sounded to me like he was bragging about it. What I mean is you would think that he thought that put him on some kind of pedestal or something, being privileged. I mean I didn't see any black and blue marks and if Gersh did give him any they were gone, healed, so it was just Dickie's word against anybody's.

6

Let me know my balance?

I had just clipped $90 out of someones pocket. A man I'd met at a urinal. Sucked his ass and when I had his pants down....it's an old story. A way of life not approved by the masses.

Look, it's making a living...my balance, please.

I then run across the street and get some H from Mike Visconti, a former italian gangster, since mellowed, feeling simply ebulient with $90 in my kick. The exact moment is where I'm at. I'm in the toilets for thrills, erotic stimulation and if any money comes my way it becomes a plus, a double positive. As long as I remain in toilets there is no need for money, but, life away from toilets has to be supported ... food, rent, drugs. A few years back, in my early teens, I often thought of bringing a lunch when visiting toilets so as not to interrupt my stay with actual physical hunger.

Let me know my balance?

---

7 A Likely Tip

There were a few people around the racetrack, around the stables is where I'd see them hobbling about with bent backs and bowlegs. I thought to myself that they must be ex-jockeys, race riders that had fell off horses or had been maybe kicked by horses but I've since found most of these people are suffering chronic back problems.

Blaming cigarettes in backrooms drinking piss at various urinals, knees scruffy. It was my left knee, my left kneecap that would give way. I explained to people, it's a trick knee I got in high school playing football. What I actually was doing was I was drinking glassfuls of piss right in front of whoever was there and I found that my action was responsible for getting people horny. Race riders, jockeys, people have told me, these same people denying they are into it, the majority of jockeys they've managed to see undressed have abnormally large cocks.

It was the cough from cigarettes that I attributed to my bad back. I'd sit on pricks after a few beers and be able to take the largest ones with no trouble. A few good mouths of spit was all that I needed. What I did at the racetrack wasn't associated with jockeys, horses or the stables, in the parking lot is where I worked and sometimes the horse owners after parking their cars would give me a likely tip on a horse race.

19

8   Swell

S ometimes, with Max, I'd sit around on doorsteps, but not as a rule. Max was I'd say roughly 70 years old, flabheavy not fat and his ankles and feet were swollen so that all he could get on his feet were carpet slippers... he had smooth skin, hairless chest and his jowls resembled a new born infants ass cheek. I'd take a look at Max, and think, he's an unmistakable old quean from way back when it was chic to lay down and smoke... anyway, the doorsteps we'd sit around on were located on East 8th Street a few buildings in from 3rd Avenue next to the sweatbaths where a lot of men working on the docks lived. What was it? two dollars a night with a restaurant on the premises if you lived there on a steady basis the management would reserve you a walk-in locker... beds upstairs and downstairs dormitory style and cubbyhole private rooms for fifty cents extra. A non-practicing medical doctor and his son, both residents of Brooklyn, owned the place.

We were inseparable one summer. I'd hear of a writing physician, give Max the fee, telling him don't come out of the office empty handed... show him your swollen feet.

I had this petty larceny shortchange con that I'd get enough money so's to cash the prescriptions Max got, to pay for our nights lodging at the sweatbaths, to eat a few chopped liver sandwiches... we'd never starve, me and Max, although food was secondary. Medicine, Max got by cashing prescriptions, sustained us..... injectible stuff.

The way our days went all worldly business we'd finish before dark then we'd check into the sweat baths prepare and inject what I was just talking about... of course we did it privately in our walk-in lockers. Everyone there is practically naked except for the management gives you a skimpy off-white jacket that just barely reaches the thighs and a 24 inch long towel... anyway, I have large testicles. I'd order the food mostly as I said the chopped liver sandwiches or occasionally omelets, salami omelets, cornbeef omelets... the fellow that ran the restaurant concession, a nickname like Eddy The Polack, it's a polish neighborhood, he was into the same type of medicine as me and Max. If we happened to seem to be falling asleep over the food we were eating Eddy The Polack would come from around his counter giving us a gentle poke... any way, when he'd give me a poke I'd adjust my testicles, not lift my head, adjust my testicles to signify my alertness.

About nine in the evening the place would start to fill up. On weekends if we wanted a bed downstairs we'd have to occupy one by at least ten oclock or else it was upstairs and the beds upstairs were a different story... anyway, times me and Max couldn't find a bed downstairs, it was hard for Max to climb the stairs, he'd lean on me. Alright, the beds upstairs, the dormitory. . . in the dormitory upstairs sleeping wasn't the big thing it was sex and that was if it wasn't for the injectible medicine, my thing. In other words sex was my thing but for that summer with all the injectible prescription medicine I was sending Max, setting him up with physicians, to get ... show him your swollen feet. What I'm saying most of the time that summer I'd be too out of it for sex, too sedated, yet actually a few times with Max lying next to me, usually three or four in the morning, upstairs, a stranger would awake me with his mouth and I never objected.

Max couldn't have missed what was going on between me and other fellows though he never let on. I wanted to confirm it so's

that we'd have more in common than the injectible medicine...
Max, you're an old quean, aren't you? Well, anyways, I never
did and it's too late. I dumped Max when I learned I could go
into physicians for my own prescriptions... my ankles and feet
were starting to swell.

———————————————————

9 Orangeburg to Macon And So Forth

Downstairs in the cellar of life exchanging rings airplane travel south. A warm climate working at stealing to support cigarette drinking various narcotics. Told me in his letter he was quiting nicotine again preparing for his latest love by swimming in the bay weather's been warm seventyfive or near eighty everyday.

Three dollar bags five dollar bags on the street drugstore stuff speed cruising toilet pickups going to his friends house for a supposedly crowd of bodies into a proper sixtynine. Next late afternoon on midway asking swinger agent copped from in the past if you holding any of that powdered meth. Orangeburg to Macon from Macon to Jacksonville from Jacksonville to Santurce. In Santurce swilling cough syrup and PG (paregoric). Planed to Boston then by automobile to Miami Beach on the nod. Sexual liaisons with prescription writing physicians one passenger in automobile that's what the passengers job was making croakers.

It was in the bus station where I met him this guy. Greyhound bus station in Charlotte through a peep hole passed notes him saying how he liked plump men. Prison discharge suit wrinkled badly when looking in mirror mens room shower food chits and a small cashiers check from a welfare organization got me home to Massachusetts. Hello hello I'm home from prison. What are you going to do? What are you going to do find a job go to work hustle jog a few miles everyday get back into the business the carnival business get hooked up to a booster as his shade? So he says to me in a letter coyly embarrassed something like I really must have my head examined not only rings but exchanging vows of fidelity.

10   Light on His Feet

Look at me now he insisted. You remember, Tony? You. remember how I was? Big, big from lifting weights. Situps, situps, doing a hundred situps in be bop alley. The toilet drinking coffee, hot coffee. Hot coffee with the rest of those guys hanging around... ever really listen to bop?

So on the strength of the above, be bop alley, the toilet, the hot coffee... it's all a lot of shit from the drug hospital, I let him, Tony... he had a younger fellow with him, take me to his friends place. Dynamite, dynamite three dollar bags up a couple of flights of stairs. After leaving... forgetful blot, choked by him his arm the fellow with him in front leading, yet, no great loss of confidence. What'd I have? What'd I blow... twentyfive dollars? Probably the kicker is it wasn't a stranger. It was someone, we were supposed to know each other, from a drug hospital.

Everybody crowds into the doorway listening... drummer what's he doing? Is it called a solo? Making noise? Technical remarks about one hand or the other being fast, fast left hand... ever really listen to bop? So, anyways defensively I wiped the episode out of my mind, but for a sore throat... I had a sore throat for a week.

Dynamite three dollar bags? An old queans rehash. Rehash...
it's about how when I got mugged a long time ago just breaking
into the carnival business, a comedy of errors. Not the carnival
business. The carnival business wasn't what I'm refering to as
being a comedy of errors. Had to jump into the city for a taste
then sucking whatever and wherever and about be bop I'd
never understood how to listen, what the heck. Earlier on I'd
been drinking whiskey so to this here Tony what was I, a
means to sustain his habit, alcohol dulling my senses? Alright,
so he and his friend mugged me and it wasn't until the next
morning I realized I didn't even have a dime to make a
telephone call... bring me a pair of pants, a clean pair of pants.
Who would know that I'd lost my pants, had purposely taken
them off seeking to drown myself in sexual activity as sort of
a balm to my mugging... sort of to ease the pain of my own self
ridicule like the time once in similar vicinity survived an
intended hotshot, robbed of serious money, seven hundred,
flashing money instead of my prick? What comes to mind,
readily, quean I knew... kissing each other with mouths full of
piss... had his cock pierced. We also knew we'd met before, but
neither one of us stood on ceremony mutual sexual tastes being
the leveler. No, now if I see a guy, a straight, I can look at them
as if they were invisible.

Of course things sure aren't what they used to be, sounds...
sounds more sophisticated and anyways my body can no longer
handle the stuff it used to handle and as far as three dollar bags
it's ancient history. The fellow, Tony, that mugged me I
couldn't even have went for sexually. The ideas they have...
situps, lifting weights or talking about it leaves me flat.

We, Steve, I and a few others gave our money, score money, to
this party, he was in his mid-seventies but still light on his feet.
Where he went to score was a poor spanish section of the city
and with him... he had pale white skin so that when he went
into this section all youngsters sitting on doorsteps knew the
guy could be in this neighborhood for only one reason, to score

26

for stuff. Well, they knew because every day for two weeks he'd been scoring for us... the way he used to say it's dangerous, dangerous, you get in and out in a hurry. So this particular afternoon he was late coming back and the first thing we thought he's run off with our money, cursing the fact that we trusted him for so long. Well the guy came back, banged up a little, but he came back, clutching the stuff, priding himself that those guys had him on the ground, punching, kicking him and he resisted, he resisted and wouldn't give them the stuff... our stuff, imagine, in his mid-seventies and able to move, still light on his feet.

11 Grind Store Agent with a capital 'F'

I think it was the end of the line for him when he fell in love with blonde Greg. Would I please do him a favor and patch it up? They'd been fighting. Both of them came into town to work a grind store on Revere Beach for Larry the fellow a few years later found locked in the trunk of his automobile, murdered. Actually the murder has no relationship to them or me... maybe it had to do with gambling, or, I wouldn't be surprised if some kind of cocaine deal went sour. What I'm getting at is no relationship to 'us' because, we, me and Johnny the grind store agent, excluding Greg, identified ourselves as Fags with a capital 'F'. Anyway, so what he wanted me to do, while he waited in the car, was run back into Sporters, the gay bar where Greg was drinking, wishy washy bleached out Greg, and tell him how his partner, the other grind store agent sitting in the car, loved him. Course we both knew Greg would never acknowledge that love. Alright, they traveled together and had sex when Greg was drunk, but, the total sum for Greg was both of them getting plenty of action. Plenty of action in the carnival business meant plenty of money.

Going back 20 years ago, playing Bridgeport, Connecticut, he bought a new black Continental, Greg and him slopping it up... they both left the midway telling me to cash out the other agents as though he could trust me to give him a good count and he could but I don't really think he believed it. Later, that same night, or was it some time the next day, I was told they had had a bad accident, both in the same hospital, maybe Greg didn't require hospitalization, though the other drove catching the brunt of the crash. A day or so later I hooked in as the shade for the Rhode Island booster, which in turn, being with the booster I rarely got a chance to be on a midway and if me and the booster did happen to show on a midway it was to sell the $300 suits we boosted, or rather, the Rhode Island booster boosted as I acted as his shade. One thing led to another and I didn't see these two grind store agents until my abrupt falling out with the booster a year and a half later. Was Greg still with him? He was and he wasn't. According to Greg, by now he despised his partner, Johnny the grind store agent, who referred to himself as Greg's lover. Greg could explain it, implying, everybody thought they knew my business, he was so sloppy, so weepy.

My problem understanding the situation is I couldn't believe people I chummed around with went for romanticism... I mean that's how blind being strung out made me.

Okay, prior to Bridgeport, Greg said, yes, sure he'd used before. It was nothing to me and I shot him a shot in the jabop. He had such good veins I should have been suspicious... who's in the room at the time but the protesting lover, grind store agent Johnny, of course Greg passed completely out of the picture with me all for dragging him in the hall toilet, this other one, the lover, horrified at my less than tactful suggestion.

Years before, early on, we knew each other from 8th Avenue, from 42nd Street, from 6th Avenue... a dollar was a dollar and none of the people we loved worked at traditional jobs. Troubles of my own dealing with a discontented affair... seems as though time flew. Suddenly released from a house of correction and it's my name being called loudly... hey, hey, well if it aint Johnny and him telling me how he's now a grind store agent. How he's now a fag in the carnival business, meaning he won't take no for an answer... meaning I should let him break me into the business. Likes to show off stuffing twenty dollar bills in my pocket... yes, honest me, saying, didn't he realize this fag, me, now only loves his junk... still goes for cock of course but loves his morning bang. Can I get serious with a person that lacks music appreciation... jazz, jazz, 1950's stuff, stuff that cooks. Huh, what? is the tight response.

It was on West 86th Street, one flight up, the room where Greg lay passed out on the floor. Johnny, I said, give me a hand dragging Greg into the hall toilet... no, he'd run downstairs to call an ambulance, so's it was left to me. Anyway, when Johnny came back I pointed, he's in there the hall toilet so he anxiously went in... what happened was Greg had stirred, had come to... we three left the room before an ambulance arrived. What did you tell me you used stuff? You've never used stuff... Greg gives me this sheepish smile... supposed to mean, big thing, so what... he was more worldly appreciating bluesy ballads, types that swing, that cook... I thought it was a joke, Johnny the grind store agent, him getting mad at me for sucking Greg's cock...

12 Those Young Spanish Queans

(for GD)

Various concessions were sent over by boat. Ticket paid for by John I flew. John and Bobby came after. No, come to think of it, Bobby and I flew together. John had a way blatantly announcing he could never trust a drug addict no matter how queer. Bobby I found completely repugnant. As it was Bobby'd end getting more money out of the proposition than John would and they were his concessions — a count store — an alibi joint — three buckets plus canvas for the whole smear. Expense money? He'd given it all to Bobby leading to big arguments trying to get my end. Straighten it out later when the show's in the air?

Anyways what really grated on my nerves soon as John arrived he hired a jeep so that he and Bobby could run around partying with young spanish queans they'd pick up both of them Bobby and John flashing fifty dollar bills ignoring me or else John whining why don't you leave the stuff alone? I'd know he'd be full of guilt for ignoring me so in that way it'd be a snap for me to get back at him by demanding more money than I was entitled to from his alibi joint, the concession I favored, while he and Bobby worked John's count store. Oh we'd meet now and then, John and I, socially, him showing off his latest pick-up one or another of those young spanish queans he was partial to. We'd drive to his ritzy hotel-cabana type accommodations next to a large swimming pool — it was

31

off season on this island —place is more or less deserted making it an ideal setting for drinking and sex bouts. I vividly recall an incident. I'm in John's, was it a suite with a refrigerator, no, that was Bobby's. Anyway John's telling one of those young spanish queans to take out his prick so that I could see what it looked like. A pretty massive hunk and I hadn't any qualms about getting down with it. There I was down with it and at the same time removing bits of my clothing. At this juncture John attempted to pull me away from this young spanish queans prick. John's smiling. He's a frozen smile on his lips but is really in a livid rage invoked by me on a prick he's invested time and money on.

Leaving stuff alone injectible or non-injectibile wasn't a question somebody not in the know personally can deal with. Drinking over-the-counter stuff, paregoric, is just as addictive as injectibiles. Limited input five two ounce bottles of stuff within a twelve hour duration. And it was hot, temperature somedays topping the hundred mark, trudging about collecting my bottles, stumbling over the native speech. Even, of all things, using pidgin english. Pidgin english, imagine what it must sound like to an islander - bottle of what did you say?

In back's all shed huts built on stilts. A partly filled marshy area. In front's a modern stadium. Sideways looking from my alibi joint's an armory constructed of what looks to be yellow stucco. Young children, barefoot boys mostly living with their families in the shed huts, clustered by my alibi joint — used as interpreters soon's I got a score from a mark I'd give a few of them, the barefoot boys, a dollar or so smash, nickels and dimes. Islanders enjoyed the same monetary standard we did where we came from. Feeling was in the beginning John seriously thought he might get rich with this off season overseas proposition - that was a big lie. Yet, looked at differently, say focusing on those young spanish queans, it can be a completely realistic proposition. And me at the time if I'd left stuff alone.

13 Crook

He was younger than me. He was Polish. He lived across the street from me. He went to parochial school. He traded comic books with me in my hall on the third floor, 76 Walnut Street. We traded comic books while people were eating supper. See who's at the door? It's Eddie with funny books and I'd get my collection. His prick with tight skin, out, where I'd have it trying to pull the tight skin back to the slit, so the slit would show where he pissed from. For an extra comic book. For ten cents, that always turned the trick. Money always got Eddie's pants down.

This here is how you lay the note I was telling Stanley. Explaining at the next stop, watch me when I buy the coffee. A couple of years before in the same area, I was with Roy then, we were being tailed. We've been fingered, Roy said. Fingered, Roy? Yes, fingered by one of those persons hanging around the bus station cafe, Roy added, elaborating. If they get a chance they'll force us off the road. Roy didn't need to say robbery was the prime motive of the people in the automobile behind us.

Day ago we'd come into this city, me and Roy, out laying the note. We occupied separate rooms in the same hotel. The hotel close to the bus station cafe. Catty corner from the bus station cafe sat the train terminal containing a quietly active mens toilet. It'd be where I'd be headed soon's I could duck Roy.

33

When you lay a note, Stanley, I told him, if you're found out act like it's an honest mistake. What Roy did he'd carry a pint of cheap wine in his hip pocket, plus, Roy'd wear a hospital identification tag on his left wrist in case he ever had a rumble.

Roy went to his room. I went to my room. My room was on a different floor below Roy. It was a four story building and the hotel didn't start until one flight up. From my room I went directly to the train terminal toilet.

Who would do that, finger us, I'd be asking Roy the next day with me driving at the same time trying to lose the automobile tailing ours? Either these people tailing us gave up or else lost sight of our automobile. Anyway, we weren't able to lay a note. It was Roy's decision, to be on the safe side, not to return to this city. What I mean is with all the excitment it became too late for either one of us to lay a note.

You can't expect to do it right from the go, Stanley, I said. Keep your eye on me when I buy a package of gum at the next gasoline stop. Roy was great on ethics, money split exactly down the middle, between those traveling together. This city is where me and Roy spent three months in jail for being suspicious out of towners. A case where Roy's hospital iden- tification tag couldn't wrangle us out of that particular di- lemma. We both were let out when it was determined there was no concrete legal basis for further incarceration.

At the train terminal by feeling underneath into the next toilet booth I met someone. It was that someone I was in bed with lying naked head to toe. The only stitch of clothing we may have had on was socks. Both of us busy in stated position, me on my back. The someone had spread his legs and my face so to speak was buried in his ass crack, when Roy, just outside the door of my hotel room, knocked and when I didn't reply to his knock began loudly calling my name. To the someone with me

I waved with my hand silently a signal to let nothing interrupt what we were doing. The fact was what we were doing was so pleasurable we both became oblivious of Roy alternately calling my name and knocking on the door.

Stanley, after you lay a note, whomever you're with don't connect until well away from the initial area. What I'm getting at, moving in said manner helps whomever you're with and yourself to stay clean. It was one of Roy's chief theories that I agreed with, staying clean, even if it meant sacrificing any money we'd accumulated. Best, too, if you dress conservatively, dark blues and grays, I instructed Stanley.

Innocently enough it so happens, the last time I saw Eddie he had placed his left forearm in the crook of his right arm the latter end held in a clenched fist. Eddie's fist obviously aimed towards me about to leave the urinal on recognizing him, Eddie, at the sink, whom I hadn't seen in at least twenty years. My intentions just to say hello Eddie, play the rest by ear. I was no longer interested in comic books. I'm sure by intuition he wasn't either. As I was about to open my mouth that's when he wriggled his clenched fist at me, his right fist, as I've said, his left forearm in its crook.

14 Meanwhile...

Wanting to admit nothing, Verbal, wanting to admit nothing verbal. Pre-carnival age running with a group of older people. Suit, tie, dice in pockets switching one pair of dice to palm at almost the same time dropping the previous pair loose. A dice mechanics job is to switch dice undetected by human eyes. Instructions from experienced older people constantly have at least two pairs of dice in pockets practicing how to switch.

Ricky perfecting his routine, a dance with a reptile, for night-club drag shows. Tell me you love me. Tell me you love me. It was Ricky's most repetitious line. Out hustling dice I'd made money. Now I was into drugs. Try as I might Ricky refused all my offers to turn him on, get him high, same as I was. I had this separate life with older people hustling dice laying groundwork for a career as a professional gambler.

I'd met Ricky in New York City, Bryant Park, the park behind the Fifth Avenue Public Library. I'm pretty sure it's where I met him and I think after we met we went to a bar close by on 6th Avenue for a drink. Although, as stated earlier, wanting to admit nothing verbal, it slopped out of me husky voiced, me telling him how much I cared for him. Tell me you love me. Tell me you love me. Like I've said already it was Ricky's often most repeated line. You mean a lot to me. You mean an awful lot to me I told him oh I don't know how many times.

Hardly did I know the proper odds on numerical combinations, betting odds shooting dice, when there I was with the group of older people, we called ourselves a dice mob, in a large picnic area near Washineton, D.C., on the shores of Chesapeake Bay, squatting down on my knees shaking and shooting dice. The event was an annual tri-state business mens club get-together. Six of us we'd faked our way in.

Ricky broke with me citing the overall reason, drug use. Yet for a short time saw me clean, that is, drug free. Hankering to patch up our differences, showing Ricky money, it may have been some of the money I'd made at the Chesapeake Bay thing, I don't know, anyways I had enough to take both of us down south for the winter. I don't remember what happened to Ricky's reptile, the six foot black snake he danced with in his nightclub act. I recall one of the spots he was booked being raided by police. Drag shows were illegal in most parts of the country then. I purposely broke with the older group of people, the dice mob, because I felt uncomfortable with them so awkward were they sexually.

Was it that season the reason surfaced it would make little difference if suddenly I became capable of saying I love you Ricky whether said matter-of-factly or with profound emotion? He'd look at me and what his look said to me it said bluntly I was full of shit. So it was the season we called it quits by mutual agreement. I had my righteous complaints and so did Ricky have his righteous complaints for once we were able to keep them to ourselves speeding up drifting apart.

B & B on the beach. Playing bankers and brokers on the beach, across from The Tidewater, using strippers, beveled decks of playing cards, bicycles. The living was easy. A good part of the time spent counting the take. It wasn't a hustle Ricky took to. Besides dancing with his black snake in drag Ricky was a specialty thief, favored burglary. Progression as a professional gambler encompassed more than a few pairs of mis-spotted dice. As I've said, Ricky, as a close companion and bed partner meant a lot to me, false it might seem when I recoiled at his demanding parroting. Tell me you love me. Tell me you love me. What I mean is he meant a lot to me and I wanted him to be a part of my various hustles, the dice, the bankers and brokers on the beach. I mean it was beyond me when consideration was given to the fact he liked money as well as I did. Alright, one thing led to another as Ricky left going north.

In those days gay relationships were never supposed to be anything other than monogamous. Anyway now I was free to sleep with anybody I chose. So began a round of gay bar hopping. Who should I meet but two queans from my Bryant Park and 8th Avenue 42nd Street days, John and Big Alice. Both of them penniless. Both living with Chips Walker the milky white skinned piano playing quean from New Orleans. We were to have a five week affair. Meanwhile...

15 Never Passed a Fix Up Never Passed a Fix Up...

S o hard put broke without a dime standing in front of and then alongside of The Garden Cafeteria. A short while before left a goofball artist his West 49th street place. This here goofball artist a total mess. Total total a complete total mess eveything sink stinking crawling with odors aromas of old and new magazines piled 4 and 5 thick around his bed sheets that haven't seen the light of daytime soap operas in at least a month of sundays.

Wearing my good blue suit my only good blue suit my case good blue hustling suit. The suit worn on the hustle to project an image of respectability. A clean button down ivy league shirt dark tie to match stockings thusly arrayed one time or another even carrying a brief a leather brief. On the 50th street side of the cafeteria by the stairs leading down to 8th avenue subways soon as a person exits my instructions were to cut into them cut into them with a story a story sort of like a mini-tragedy stolen billfold hospital visit anything anything to evoke a sympathetic ear short of a blow by blow description of your 24 electric shock treatments in a state run institution tell them you need subway fare money for phone calls to help alleviate frantic situation.

Happened 3 bags earlier full of H cop harness cop on patrol beat said hey you where you from taken by suprise so suddenly barely enough a second or two stuffed bags in my mouth my mouth with no intentions of swallowing the shit unless the harness cop became suspicious and decided to physically pry open my mouth. Anyway managed a muted mumble the cop in turn answered me with a growled well then go back to where you belong.

The goofball artist his story roughly peopled private wealth send him a check monthly and a seperate check to the owner of the building where he lives for the rent is the way it was heard. The rental check to the owner of the building is never late but the goofball artist his check sometimes it comes on time and sometimes it seems like it'll never come especially especially wide awake awake completely wide awake no nembutals tuinals seconals nothing subject to fits of depressions wingding seizures,

So hard put dime stand cafeteria wearing good blue suit trying to bum carfare downtown expected wired moneygram thirty dollars not again not again not you again. Rolled into city literally in Buick 1950 Buick motor humming but brakes shot shot right to the floorboards absolutely nothing stops planned at least one hundred yards in advance managed fifty dollars for the hulk at automobile junkshop in Coney Island vicinity. Motor humming but brakes shot look at the rubber look at the rubber brand new rubber with set of dated papers for proof. Doridens white pills grooved down the middle after going through 5000 yellow capsuled nembutals rolled into the city from west coast on the mysterious lam from nothing really that anyone can put a legal finger on driving day and night day and night drug sick with guilt drug sick with guilt and nowhere to score until literally rolling into the city two weeks later from the west coast back to the east coast a little sex here and there on road at rest stops I suppose though nothing leaving a lasting memory of same.

So broke standing with hard put dimes good blue hustling suit kept spiffy neatly pressed while you wait at 24 hour shop even if it meant spending my last cent to avoid jail knowing police approach crummy looking people first. Walked away from downstairs out the door goofball artist left me reflective the dirt the poverty of monthly checks written more to keep him hidden than for actual life sustaining support. He himself the goofball artist he dreads visits from his people with private wealth they have him locked up in properly sterile clean sheeted institutions don't let him out of your sight don't let him out of your sight manipulative type manipulative type. Records documented in black and white notarized signatures easy to remember but so hard to forget.

Flops flops seventyfive cent flops secret is not to remove clothes if valued nudity is to be kept meaning once undressed don't expect same clothing back. The person that introduced me to the goofball artist he had all the stuff about the flops the price the clothes down pat where to stand hard put next to The Garden Cafeteria dimes saved increase change. It was summer summer he knew everybody and everybody knew him on the scene on the scene on the scene that is they knew him and he knew them. Never passed a fix up never passed a fix up...

16 Right From The Can Itself

Queans we knew me and Hush wandering the street the streets hustling parks haunting parks stealing breakfast rolls left in doorways of groceries. Shook our respective heads stealing cash lamps jewelry off of trusting pickups lead up flights of dark halls.

How much how much? How much do you charge? What do you do what do you do? I do everything everything for five dollars ten dollars all night while Hush slept I'd slip out at six in the morning wearing my jogging suit to look for strangers panting for sex. Fast sex fast sex one two three one two three and it'd be over back with Hush issuing an affectionate wet kiss telling Hush whispering I got rolls fresh rolls fresh rolls. Back in bed under the covers with Hush he'd expect something to be shaking as a matter of speaking sexual sexual getting it on in the morning it being only natural after abstaining all night. Did I dare explain that when I was supposed to be jogging on the bridle path avoiding horse manure what I really was doing was was repeating performances performances going down on practically anybody willing to drop their trousers or zip open their flies. It'd be alright actually if it were done for money money was one thing but doing it for love definitely was not permissible.

Hush and Freddie, 1949

The whole bit is to be ever alert alert in order to rob anything of value left unattended lamps in shops jewelry billfolds holding cash again and again Hush the B & E specialist myself drifting along trying unsuccessfully to develop a lucrative confidence game. Your stick your stick what's your stick was an expression later used to mean what you did to earn a living. Uptown to the fence having a very small room on 7th Avenue abutting 110th Street. Jimmy Jimmy Tyler Jimmy'll buy anything whether he needs it or not as long as it's stolen property. This time a lamp Hush clipped as it sat like a statue in a mid-city store window near the famous millionaires plaza containing an ice skating rink for ice skating queans. Many queans and there is no mistake about them being queans skating round and round the rink every now and then a more adroit quean carving a figure eight but always queans queans in the winter skating ice skating in the rink located in the plaza owned or named for a famous millionaire. At Jimmy's small room Jimmy offering puffs of sweet smelling smoke we don't we don't Hush and I we concentrate on sucking and fucking sucking and fucking that's our stick primarily sucking and fucking five dollars a shot ten dollars all night. A rough way a rough way a rough way to go sometimes we'd argue continuously half the night trying to remember people banging on the floor upstairs downstairs shutup you two be quiet. He took the lamp giving us a good price shaking his head from side to side professing not to understand why he buys this stuff. Offhand a few years later inquiring of somebody did they know Jimmy Tyler the Jimmy Tyler that lived on 7th Avenue abutting 110th Street in a small room in a large elevator building. Yes they knew Jimmy Tyler they were sure it was the same Jimmy Tyler doing time for a federal drug bust. Yes me and Hush knew Jimmy Tyler I'm sure Jimmy'd remember me and Hush two queans refusing puffs of sweet smelling smoke those too queans stealing any anything they could lay their hands on.

The Residence Club The Residence Club The Mens Residence Club we lived there for a while me and Hush did where some of our most vehement arguments took place over the silliest notions concerning love and loyal physical attachments. Talk about lamps stolen lamps massive affairs crashing shattered on the floor against walls glass smashing glass we always had plenty of lamps about heavy based lamps yet at the front desk at the front desk Hush and I maintained a friendly relationship with all clerks on the front desk both day and night wandering in smiling a pleasant greeting as far as I can remember that is.

Down the street a block and a half. Actually around the corner from The Mens Residence Club down 8th Avenue a block and a half was the well known Stillman's Gymnasium where professional boxers trained daily daily everyday every afternoon in fact up the flight of stairs to Stillman's Gymnasium I'd go change to my gym clothes then I'd loosen up shadow box shadow box maybe four or five three minute periods resting a minute in between then I'd be called by one of the many trainers to get ready for a sparring session a sparring session in one of the two rings at Stillman's Gymnasium. Hush Hush I'd ask Hush come on up to Stillman's Gymnasium? Hush come on up and watch me spar? It was my sparring sessions with other boxers that I wanted Hush to watch shadow boxing punching the heavy bag light bag speed bag doing situps and bends stuff like that didn't mean much but sparring I wanted Hush to watch me sparring with other boxers because someone close to me had to appreciate my finesse sparring. I knew the regulars at Stillman's Gymnasium watched me had their eyes on me when I sparred though it didn't count it didn't count at all unless it could be Hush. For approval approval apparently it seems where Hush had to approve of a lot of the things I did. He never came to Stillman's Gymnasium to watch me spar. Hush would look at me and sneer you you're always looking at mens cocks. Basket gazing basket gazing Hush would say over and over again you you're always basket gazing at mens cocks. No I'm not no I'm not not all the time no I'm not always basket gazing at mens cooks is what I'd occasionally answer Hush whenever I tired of hearing it repeated so many times basket gazing basket gazing.

Stoop that low stoop that low that anybody could stoop that low to actually open a can of catfood and eat the can of catfood Hush told me about a quean Hush knew that was staying at another queans house and obviously hungry there must not have been any food around this queans house where this quean Hush knew was staying only the can of catfood and that quean just boldly opened a can of catfood with a can opener and ate it ate it in front of all these other queans who were there and saw this quean Hush knew actually eat. The way Hush put it the quean ate the food right from the can itself.

---

17 and Fish Gotta Fly

I t's a different world a different world today than my time back in the early 1950s. There was the music of course be bop jazz it just coming in to its own listening much too intently listening to hard not hearing much more than noise blaring noise capsuls gelatin capsuls selling for two dollars apiece three for five three gelatin capsuls filled with horse fairly decent horse for five dollars.

Hush. Hush got his nightclub act together doing an exotic dance in drag with a black snake. On and off again with Hush when it was felt by me finally that Hush could be put up with only as long as I had my junk figuring down deep if Hush took his first fix of stuff we'd meet again as old lovers like we once were at the beginning enjoying simple things rolls and cream cheese in the morning. Here was some really good shit really good horse and it was way beyond me Hush didn't want it Hush wasn't having any of it. Innocent though it may sound I figured the way I figured it was whereas I liked the stuff why shouldn't Hush like it in fact I was sure I was sure once Hush had a taste it would be the answer for both of us what I mean is making a go of it our love affair making a go of it was very important to me sex too but sex wasn't all that encompassing anymore with me a loving relationship corny though it might sound to me bred from familiarity oh it was mixed up mixed up the shit the really good shit. A chance to deal to deal shit me and Hush equal partners wasn't I already going into the city and buying a couple of ounces a week living with Hush again bagging the stuff in his apartment the basement apartment on Village street with the snake in its basket on the pipes near the ceiling the hot water pipes it likes the heat it likes the heat Hush said that's why I got it up on the pipes. The snake was up on the pipes every once and awhile I'd go out and walk around the neighborhood by prearrangment I told people I thought could be trusted at certain hours I told them I'd be on so and so street no no definitely not no they couldn't have my address. No I wouldn't go for that I assured Hush as long as we're living together no one gets our address. I knew Hush wanted to make money I knew that about Hush I knew that and if we were making money both of us together I figured heck won't that make our love affair last. So anyways at certain hours I'd be selling sometimes capsuls of shit or as would happen occasionally running out of gelatin capsuls I'd bag the shit in cellophane.

About the rolls and cream cheese in the morning a throw away thing a piece of nostalgia how like one time how we used to go shopping together when we lived in the city it predates the junk on 9th avenue we used to go always looking for a bargain always like maybe really cheap hamburger so cheap that when we'd fry it it would fry away to nothing well the hamburger was for to be poured over rigatoni in a tomato sauce we were so proud both of us between ourselves about our Italian tomato sauce it gets better everyday Hush said and I said it too I said it too it'll be better tomorrow and even better the next day. Hamburger trovvi hamburger trovvi Hush would order whenever we ate out hamburger trovvi that's raw hamburger with onions salt and pepper at least I think that's what goes into it. I didn't know I couldn't figure it how Hush could eat raw hamburger I'd ask how can you eat raw hamburger Hush? Shows myself how innocent I was.

The drug dealing bit? Alright Hush couldn't take it not the

actual dealing he was all for that the money the money coming in steady it was myself on stuff get away from me get away from me your high Hush said and I'd answer listen Hush I'm the same person the exact same person I always was. The way I figured it I figured Hush was using the idea that because I got high on stuff I was a different person it left me dumbfounded dumbfounded so to speak. For me it all boiled down to wait until Hush gets curious enough to try the stuff then I'd say Hush see didn't I tell you isn't it great isn't the shit great Hush we'd embrace we'd embrace and everything between us me and Hush would be fine fine both of us nodding nodding talking to each other in husky whispers.

Alright so Hush never was curious enough about stuff to try it and soon dampers were put on my dealing bit when these two cops I still remember their names Chisolm & Gibbons these two narcotic cops that's what they were known as narcotic cops both of them with identical florid beefy looking faces I never could figure out which one of them was Chisolm and which one of them was Gibbons it didn't matter anyways because they were they always seemed to be like inseparable twins Chisolm and Gibbons if I seemed to be seeing them both around wherever I was at near Hush's basement apartment or close by Village street then there was no mistaking they had to be on to me on to me that I was dealing horse. One day lucky for me one day on a whim when I was supposed to go deliver some stuff to someone a person who'd already paid me in advance incidentally it's the way I did business getting paid in advance just as a precaution in case say the money was marked if something did come off and I was searched the marked money wouldn't be on my person so one day on a whim right before I was to go make a delivery I said Hush Hush go to so an so street corner and see if it looks fairly safe nobody among my buyers knew Hush nor did the two narcotic cops Chisolm & Gibbons. So of course what happens Hush comes back down to the apartment in a few minutes and said there's these two beefy guys in a doorway right across from where your buyer is waiting and

Hush goes on to describe them and I said Hush Hush that's
Chisolm & Gibbons yes Hush Chisolm & Gibbons the narcotic
cops.

Later on sometime Hush gave up dancing with the snake I
don't know if it was right after I gave up dealing drugs or what
anyways it was about that time the time Hush saw Chisolm &
Gibbons anyways I had this thing where this person I knew a
few years before we were in the service we both got thrown out
and I was a young real hotshot hustler when we were in the
service. So anyways he called me up and I said hello exchanging pleasantries and I said this is a surprise you're the last
person I expected to call me what's up what's up what's going
on. Anyways he was down south at a popular resort making
money hand over fist so to speak hand over fist and it was right
up my alley he figured gambling using phoney cards and dice
just like when we were in the service so anyways I said alright
alright I'm coming down there he wanted to know did I need
money he'd send me money to go down there no no I said I don't
need any I'll be down there though I told him. Again me and
Hush on the verge of breaking up or had broke up for all I
remember so I went to Hush and I said Hush look it I'm going
south to this here popular resort so you want to come do you
want to go with me Hush and Hush answered yes sure yes he'd
go with me. Anyways I was elated really elated that Hush was
going with me here it was I thought it was all over with us
practically over and no it wasn't over no it wasn't over yet.

18 Saltier Today...

Thing behind me's a fan blowing on my back. Know what I mean, Peter? These people, ones we knew close, shot up with many times, married, so to speak, to the clinics, the clinics. And their lives they don't have any control over. It's the clinics, they belong to the clinics. So, so that's why when you asked me what about the clinics? You jumped at me saying you had to shower on account of the ocean being exceptionally salty today. I felt the same way, agreeing with you, ocean's a lot more saltier today than yesterday...

19 Three Years Six Months and Nine Days

Bridgeport is where the show was Amusements of America. Midway located across from the ocean beach to take a fast duck in in the afternoon let's go swimming let's go swimming also a heavily cruised toilet downtown in an old fashioned railroad station one gay bar nearby and a room at the Y paid for daily.

I wasn't driving my own automobile yet. Soon's I got off the bus there was a message for me the show's in Bridgeport I forget how I got to Bridgeport by train probably from Boston so right away is why soon's I got off the train first or one of the first things I did after dumping my bag in a locker was look for the men's room sign alright so that's why I knew this is the spot I'll spend a lot of my leisure time. Next thing I did was hire a taxi to take me to the midway slim and trim me slim and trim after a short while before completing three years six months and nine days in prison.

Well hello hello look who's here look who's here and look look he looks so wonderful wonderful Freda looks so wonderful my pet name among queans in the carnival business Freda for Fred he and she or her interchangable. We can't get over it really me and Al how wonderful you look after doing how much time three years six months and nine days in prison in prison hey everybody here's Freda just out of the joint. No kidding no kidding Freda you look wonderful wonderful almost as good as you looked ten years ago when you and Hush were going together and I was going with Joey remember Joey and Al and Al Miss Al was picking up sailors on 42nd street blowing them blowing them beating them up if they got nasty.

Hush when's the last time you seen Hush Freda when's the last time you seen her? Did you know that did you know Miss Al went with Hush before you went with her with Hush yes. So we went and I got a room at the Y it was a big Y with plenty of available rooms on weekends on weekends that's when the place could be counted on for activity sexual activity action. After that same night when the last mark straggled off the midway come on let's go to the bar the gay bar downtown so with Al and this other quean who thought she was my sponsor because she once got me her lawyer friend to defend me her lawyer friend who helped get me get me three years six months and nine days. Freda's back Freda's back no kidding you look wonderful wonderful then I explained how I used to jog jog everyday in prison jog around the prison yard practically everyday everyday jog two miles everyday sometimes five five miles cocks cocks sucking lots of pricks oh plenty of pricks plenty of them everyday everyday everynight everynight I had a lineup of guys guys that wanted their pricks sucked and of course accomodating Freda. That's it that's it I said to myself I'm not going to come out of prison looking lumpy lumpy so little by little I built this thing where everynight I had these guys lined up waiting for me waiting for me to suck their pricks in my cell they'd wait sort of lined up sitting on my bed each cell had its own individual outside area in the rear a small enclosure a small enclosure it's where I took these guys in orderly fashion one after another and they were so well behaved so well behaved thanking me thanking me when I finished with each of them Freda Freda we don't know what we'd ever do without you. How wonderful she looks doesn't she look wonderful everyday I said practically everyday I'd jog two miles sometimes as much as five miles it's why it's why to this quean who thought she was my sponsor it's why I look so wonderful so wonderful when the lights went out this is after the early lineup our cells were left open wide open this was minimum security we queans we known queans all worked on the farm and at night our cells were left wide open from cell to cell from cell to cell bed hopping was common and me you know me you know aggressive Freda you know she got most of the action earlier earlier on it was sucking lots of sucking but once the lights were out if anything that's the time the fucking took place the actual fucking this one number this one number like I'd sit on his prick literally sit on his prick facing his face facing his face looking into his eyes while I sat on his prick and he humped up and down up and down and he had no choice but to look back look back into my eyes returning looks into each others eyes anyways soon's I felt his prick was in my ass for a complete fuck a complete fuck literally well I'd jerk off jerk off facing his face looking into his eyes and you know how you know how a quean knows when a prick's just about ready to come to come in a queans ass well don't you think Freda would shoot her load all over this numbers chest all over this numbers chest at the same instant I'd feel the first throb of his come in my ass know what I mean how a quean feels a numbers prick throbbing its come up her ass honey oh up Freda's ass honey so I wasn't going to come out of prison lumpy lumpy from inactivity so I made up my mind that like I said I'd jog everyday practically.

20 Something Else Entirely

Mutt & Jeff the newspapers called them one's tall one's short. Bandits their real names the tall one was Kelly and the shorter one was Murphy and they both managed The Moss Bar located on the uptown side of 8th Avenue between 42nd and 43rd Streets NYC a gay bar and both of them Kelly and Murphy were themselves gay although I can't swear to Murphy's sexual proclivities. Kelly though Kelly and Johnny Hagen little Johnny Hagen a quean I knew a quean I had slept with more than a few times in spite of the fact Hush and I were a steady couple anyway Johnny Hagen and Kelly were supposedly lovers. Everyone was sneaking around sleeping with this one or that one nobody was supposed to know anything at all like Johnny Hagen and I would use this queans apartment this quean lived closeby on 43rd Street going crosstown towards 9th Avenue it would happen so casually maybe Hush wasn't around maybe out turning a trick and Kelly wasn't I don't think the jealous type but if Bob was around Bob was one of these legitimate business guys replete with suburban home in New Jersey secret ties to a family and all that shit but if Bob was around Bob was madly in love with Johnny Hagen he'd pay all of Hagens bills plus take him everywhere make sure he had cash on hand so if Bob was around me and Hagen wouldn't allude to sex anyway when Bob was around on occasion we'd all go bar hopping Hush and me and Bob and Hagen and Bob of course paid for everything beer and liquor Kelly Kelly never took part in these excursions Kelly was all business running the bar running the bar The Moss Bar on 8th Avenue him and Murphy Mutt & Jeff. Mutt & Jeff bandits the daily newspapers referred to them as as in a familiar frontpage headline Mutt & Jeff bandits terrorize westside merchants.

When it came out that they got caught the Mutt & Jeff bandits and that their real names their given names were Kelly the taller of the two and the other one the shorter one was Murphy we were all of us that hung around The Moss Bar we were more than a little surprised we were aghast aghast at the idea that Kelly and Murphy could be in reality the Mutt & Jeff bandits. For myself these were people I knew that I'd see everyday I may not have been on intimate terms with them although I was sneaking around having sex with Kelly's steady Johnny Hagen lots of people regulars that came into The Moss Bar were shaking their heads saying poor little Johnny Hagen poor little Johnny Hagen I don't know if it bothered me much that much that I worried about Johnny Hagen. Had to watch my step with Hush a good part of the time I wanted to end it to break up with Hush his jealousy his blind jealousy his drunken rages his suicide attempts so I was meeting numbers on the quiet along Central Park West along the walk outside of the park itself the walk lined with benches meeting these different numbers and going home with them when I knew Hush wasn't around and of course still Johnny Hagen once in awhile and even one time the blonde drag quean star Titanic the same Titanic that worked at the Club 181 of course Hush wasn't suspicious of me making it with people we actually knew Hush thought all the people I made it with were strangers casual pickups well that was a lie if there ever was one.

Can't be quite sure about events dates it could have been when I first slept with Johnny Hagen me and Hush had not gelled as an inseparable couple that may have taken a few months before we moved in together so it might be an exaggeration on my part the thing me worried Hush'd find out Johnny Hagen and me used this here queans Dick Dick Corberts apartment on 43rd street. This here quean Dick he was a set designer and an actor although not a well known personality to the general theatre going public the theatre people on Broadway knew him and taking into account what he and a friend of his another quean said that the reason he wasn't working in any Broadway stage productions at the time was that if the casting people knew you were a quean you were automatically excluded. This here was the early 1950's. Alright alright so as far as I know that was the end of Kelly and Johnny Hagens affair and also Kelly and Murphy were no longer associated with The Moss Bar a new manager took over but the same crowd still hung out there a new face would pop in and soon become a regular.

Alex was a new face for a couple of weeks. Where they come from suddenly here they are at The Moss Bar sitting in booths with their particular crowd around them like a well established institution. They all just got out of jail a lot of them a heck of a lot of them even Hush even Hush come to think of it did his 18 months in a New York State reformatory discharged 17 years old enlisting in the navy the United States Navy a sailor a sailor a gay sailor with a large pronounced cock showing through bell bottoms blues and whites blues and whites whites in the summer and blues in the winter special custom made dark blue gaberdines. What we'd do me and Hush between 7th Avenue and 8th Avenue on 42nd Street we'd look for gullible people soldiers sailors marines anything so to speak wearing a uniform three or four of them together was a good setup for us it was me did the approaching asking them what were they looking for what were they looking for what type of thrills sex were they looking for sex did they want sex for a price a reasonable price in that case yes me and my friend can provide a place where they can go where everything goes everything goes do you want to fuck do you want to watch everything anything a regular circus it was all the come on the place the whole smear fictitious me and Hush we'd have hotel keys we'd get them whenever a trick of ours hired a room so when we'd finish with the trick we'd keep the key rarely if ever did a trick want to keep the room themselves zipped fly and they'd be gone so me and Hush we'd hold on to the keys for example The Dixie Hotel. The Dixie had two entrances plus a lower basement a bus station known as The Dixie Bus Station and it served mainly The Trailway Bus line and the toilet was always crowded jammed packed jammed packed it seemed all against the urinals jerking off or softly stroking stroking it softly so the main entrance to The Dixie Hotel was on 42nd Street and we could walk right through me and Hush and exit on 43rd Street so it was ideal showing potential dupes a key to a room in The Dixie implying yes it's a suite of rooms yes sex no you pay first you pay us then we take you up the elevator flashing the key always flashing the key at them telling them what a great deal they were getting cheap cheap something like a drop in the bucket $20 for instance or actually anything we could or I could wring from them invariably with me doing the talking Hush and I would get the money then I'd lead them to the elevator let them get on first then quickly I'd thrust the key on them and just as quickly step back into the lobby as the elevator door closed and me and Hush we'd beat it out of there in a hurry out the 43rd street exit maybe gleefuly grinning if we were successful these were our happiest moments together. So that was one of our hustles whenever we got hold of a hotel key or two of course it had to be a busy place with multi exits in one door and out the other so to speak anyways all this stuff took place right around the corner from The Moss Bar so one day when Hush wasn't with me one way or another I got talking to Alex sitting in one of the booths at The Moss Bar he was drinking probably beer I was probably drinking a coke or a 7up oh I didn't drink much then rarely rarely maybe a beer once a week otherwise soft stuff cokes and 7ups. So anyways Alex is rubbing my leg kissing me on the neck I think someone warned me he goes with this really really jealous spanish quean and it was true it was true because I knew this spanish quean and this quean was madly madly in love with Alex so

58

anyways we ended going to set designer actor Dick Corberts place same place I went with Hagen it was easy Dick was mostly always in The Moss Bar and he was always agreeable in fact he got me in bed himself a few times nothing special though but with Alex it was pretty nice only thing was we had to worry word wouldn't get back to this spanish quean. I didn't want any trouble and neither did Alex so anyways that's as far as it went maybe twice twice that I went to Dick Corberts apartment to suck off Alex suck off Alex's big Polish cock he had that type of cock an uncircumsized big loose foreskinned Polish cock and I could see no wonder this spanish quean was so wildly in love with Alex. Alright so everything doesn't end here. What happened was that Alex had my name and phone number in his address book. I was clean having not yet thrown my lot in with Hush our affair was still in its initial stages not yet thievery for thievery's sake alone. Alright so Alex got picked up by the cops the cops accusing Alex of robbing the Park Avenue apartment belonging to the Roses that's Eleanor and Billy Rose Billy Rose a well known Broadway producer Eleanor Rose the former Eleanor Holms Olympic gold medal swimmer then for a long while B movie personality anyway when their apartment got robbed it generated a lot of publicity with Billy Rose going on radio and television appealing to the people that were responsible for robbing their apartment to please please if you have an ounce of decency give yourselves up give yourselves up to the police and return our property the property being a two foot square steel safe containing among other things Billy Roses favorite pearl handled gold plated 25 caliber automatic pistol. Actually it's unimportant all these details what's important to me anyways is that this caper Alex was accused of this caper had its start in The Moss Bar where good luck or bad luck would have it the Roses valet or house-boy as Billy Rose put it my houseboy my houseboy when me and Eleanor got home we found our houseboy bound and gagged the place ransacked the safe gone the safe that con-tained among other things my famous pearl handled gold plated 25 caliber automatic pistol so anyways the houseboy a west indian quean used to spend his leisure time in The Moss Bar and in The Moss Bar the Roses houseboy met a friend of Alex's a guy called Blackie and when the Roses weren't home he'd have Blackie come over he'd entertain this here Blackie and it seems Alex and Blackie and a few others from their immediate group that hung in The Moss Bar what they had in common with each other was that they knew each other from prison so what happened what took place what took place one day when Blackie had a date with the west indian quean at the Roses apartment Blackie had this plan worked out with Alex that Alex would come by the Roses apartment I'm not sure of exact details but anyways they'd made it up beforehand how they'd tie and gag the houseboy and pull off the robbery. After all this shit so to speak was over and done with the people in The Moss Bar the regulars the regulars in The Moss Bar tried to make it appear as though the west indian quean was in reality not a victim himself of the robbery but a co-conspirator along with Alex and Blackie of course that was a lot of hooey. A lot of hooey that's a lot of fucken crap some of those in the know would say. Anyways to make a long story short because the cops had Alex's address book and my name was in it so now even though the cops had Alex they didn't have Blackie this despite Billy Rose still going on radio and television and now thinking he knew who he was dealing with making intimate pleadings on a first name basis with Blackie Blackie Blackie please give yourself up please please something like save your immediate family the heartache or similar puke evoking language although personally I never bothered to listen I know it's what this here Billy Rose was saying. So anyways yours truely me I got picked up pulled in by the cops that maybe you know I was this here Blackie they were looking for so they brought me to the precinct the 47th street precinct where they had Alex and he must of said no no that's not Blackie. They'd beat him pretty bad his head seemed swollen twice its size his arms were covered with a mass of red welts he was sitting six feet away from me managing not to show a flicker of recognition towards me but he did I forget how get a rolled wad of paper to me with a telephone number and after the cops turned me loose what else could they do I called the phone number explaining to the people on the other end of the line how the cops had Alex and he needs help and a lawyer or words to that effect and they said yes yes they already knew all that so that was that and a few days later at The Moss Bar talk had died down about Alex and Blackie and the west indian quean the Roses houseboy.

The above scenes Mutt & Jeff bandits sex with Johnny Hagen sex with Alex and my eventual involvment with the cops trying to pin if they possibly could the Billy Rose thing on me if only because my name and phone number showed up in Alex's address book was all sort of fading out being a regular at The Moss Bar and of course as soon as Hush and I got a place together a place on 71st street a block and a half from central park like we both of us me and Hush we were outgrowing The Moss Bar so anyways we started going to The Silver Rail on 6th Avenue and its sister bar The Terrace around the corner on 45th street owned by the same people jewish gangster people not gay but at least hip enough to hire gay people so it wasn't really too long before me and Hush were regulars at The Silver Rail Bar and The Rails sister bar The Terrace The Moss Bar though The Moss Bar was something else entirely.

21 | In Other Words

In other words in other words Dutch would say in other words to a mark on the midway in other words this time if you win take back your money all the money you've spent in other words hitching up his pants squirming his neck around all your money back and the prize if you win in other words in other words words words Dutch would repeat take the ball swing the ball swing the ball and knock down the bowling pin emphysema coughing drooling gagging where he couldn't barely catch his breath phlegm spit and snot dribbling down his shirt front taking a swig of bourbon whiskey not in front of the joint not on the midway later on in the automobile either first the red Marlin the red Marlin the American Motors experimental sports sedan or later on later on smashed to smithereens in Georgia in Atlanta in the outskirts of Atlanta looking for the baths the gay baths so the next morning the next morning picking out an Oldsmobile an Oldsmobile a really fine running automobile cheap cheap eight or nine hundred lacking proper papers papers bill of sale and stuff like that headed for Macon Macon Georgia Macon's bus station toilet gloryhole desegregated one fifth one fifth at a time of really good bourbon good bourbon in other words in other words Dutch would say in other words you wont get sick you wont get sick drinking really good bourbon hundred proof bourbon hundred proof bourbon one fifth at a time on the dresser in Macon Georgia. In other words in other words Dutch would explain in other words I'm not Dutch at all I'm German I'm German I was born in Germany and came over here in other words when I was very young and when I was ten years old they sent me back to live with my grandmother with my grandmother on a farm in Germany warm milk from cows just milked chickens good food plenty of food in other words in other words it was The Polack The Polack that started calling me Dutch The Polack with a big prick a huge prick take the ball swing the ball knock down the bowling pin swing the ball and knock down the bowling pin smoking the same brand cigarettes as The Polack filters low tar low nicotine hard to drag on drag on in other words Dutch would repeat repeat on the midway in front of a joint in other words when you knock the bowling pin down with the ball the swinging ball you get your money back all your money back you've spent plus a prize in other words.

22 Clean Clean As A Whistle

I'd look in I'd look in on the stem I was where they advertised a famous jazz drummer poolroom upstairs couple of doors away billiards it was called a billiard parlor all carried their own pool sticks cues downstairs the subway toilet 50th street a local stop my name was on the wall taking on all comers large or small old or young hotel room number telephone welfare hotel midtown mostly for those recently discharged from state run institutions had stuff stashed in checkroom for over three months wrote them the checkroom while away please hold on to my stuff you know sort of like a certificate of consent be so kind as to because he's getting out soon as he can't be held forever can he seafood seafood poo rack a saki poo rack a saki ever hear that one held in a mental institute a mental institute for drug addicts and at the time only one felony conviction only one felony conviction held against him so I said to this here person at the reception desk say I'd really like to get onto the maintenance program the maintenance program for drug addicts a program that seems to work well for confirmed drug addicts going on to explain how I was actually certifiably a confirmed drug addict yes then sort of casually mentioned various institutions I'd been stuck in and was told sorry we don't have or we're not set up to care for your type it was sanity being questioned caught me dumbfounded awe struck reach out just reach out and slap this number in the face thirty dilaudids — thirty dilaudids I had stashed in the checkroom where at the Y the Sloane House Y in the checkroom and listen I was clean clean as a whistle so to speak only just discharged having a hotel room a welfare hotel room on W47th street guys calling up from the 50th street subway toilet wanting to meet me did I like to get beat did I like to get pissed on plus besides the thirty dilaudids there was speed and goofballs tuinals and meth tuinals and meth tuinals and meth everything carefully wrapped in one of my two bags checked in the checkroom of the Sloane House Y the Sloane House Y for over three months until my then recent discharge from the mental institute for drug addicts.

23 Both Dead and Buried

I was in my early teens it was summer and I was working with my dad helping him paint gas stations he worked for Maloney the painting contractor dad got paid according to various items he painted for instance a gas pump paid 75¢ or replacing a logo and painting the trim on a sign would pay say 90¢ sometimes we'd paint a complete gas station building signs pumps and everything else in sight. It was at that time I found out my dad was really truely insane of course at the time I wasn't able to articulate the fact that he was insane all I was capable of doing was run to my mother telling her saying in a weepy voice ma I don't want to work with daddy ma I don't want to work with him ma and of course she was a hopeless case herself laying on her back in a hospital waiting to give birth to her fourth child her first pregnancy in nine years it was a mistake a mistake I overheard a relative remark they themselves my mother and father were incredulous when the doctor confirmed my mothers pregnancy. I have this hazy remembrance of them being secretive in front of their children talking sometimes pig latin sometimes a halting yiddish.

It's only now with them both dead and buried that I have a clear picture of their insanity and their willingness to infect their children with that very same insanity infect their children by assocciation. So anyways Hush sat on the curbstone

66

downstairs and my mother pipes up with he's crying he's weeping and he's saying between sobs he won't leave until you talk to him. Don't interfere ma don't interfere so anyways the cops came and took Hush away I suppose they'd figure he belongs in a mental hospital of course I didn't give a hoot I didn't care I'd had it two years living with Hush and I'd had it. He's sitting in the gutter literally in the gutter the poor thing my mother said sobbing sobbing his eyes out. Get off my ear ma get off my ear is what I wanted to tell my mother what does she know what does she know what it's all about how me and Hush we'd suck cocks and assholes in public toilets stealing wallets out of different men's pockets while they had their trousers unsuspecting down around their ankles.

She'd say to me she'd say she'd say I want you to see a psychiatrist an analyst an analyst I want you to go to an analyst ever since I was thirteen or fourteen years old she'd been carping on and on about how she wanted me to go to a psychiatrist every now and then I'd counter with ma why don't you go you go to a psychiatrist she'd smirk back at me oh I don't need one I don't need one. Oh she was scared of herself her thoughts her homicidal leanings you know what she'd say to me on occasion you know what I'd answer what ma what am I supposed to know then she'd come out with it you you ought to be shot shot do you hear me you ought to be shot shot for the way I act she said put against some wall and shot by a firing squad I think she meant. Definitely definitely she was insane insane no more saner than my father and really really I knew how insane he was.

24 Amusements of America

Young guys young men you know fourteen fifteen sixteen coming down to the midway with stuff to sell radios TVs blenders electrical stuff just clipped and we people we agents in front of our joints maybe an item worth ninety a hundred we people we agents would offer a ten dollar bill here you want it take it or leave it they all had habits ten dollars enough for a couple of bags black veins tracks scar tissue from when the needles clogged strike a match and heat the clogged blood to unclog it and not bothering to clean off the sulphur soot from the needle then getting a hit in a vein and the soot the black sulphur soot gets under the skin leaving a black mark forever forever maybe someday they tattoo something over their tracks mother or fathers gravestone marker in prison thats why I could always tell a dope fiend where the tattoos are and Im usually right theyre covering up old tracks I mean you know Im a dope fiend myself if anybody should know what their talking about.

Young guys like I said young men irish for the most part a few spanish it was right off of Third Avenue and a 138th Street where we were holed up so to speak the show the show Amusements of America nobody said to us we agents you people you agents youve got to stay I mean if I didnt have a habit myself what I mean is staying in the city its where the best drugs were anyway its where I got one of my best pieces of flash a small expensive leather cased radio from one of them for five dollars like I said take it or leave it irish skinny I could easily have took his pants down if I hadnt had my own habit to contend with take it or leave it I said five dollars for the radio so along comes this other guy a middle aged man a looker sort of walking the midway gawking smiling friendly a potential mark and I just bought the radio admiring it the bargain I got an outright steal anyway its a hot sweltering end of July day and I couldnt believe it I couldnt believe it hes walking down the midway by all the joints and none of the agents are trying to call him in I mean I got so excited I was holding my breath waiting for him to come by my joint hoping no one had the good sense to grab him before me and finally here he was in front of me I sighed let out my breath and said to him hey mister excuse me pardon me mister you know very politely sir can I show you how this gosh dern game works I dont want your money I said keep your money in your pocket the rest was ancient history flashing the radio at him for starters anyway it was a five hundred dollar score end of July hot sweltering day take it or leave it and I still owned the piece of flash the radio.

25 **Around Town Jack**

W ay before oh it was way before that I ever even thought about using shit or smoking anything other than tobacco that was a bother where what I was supposed to be a professional athlete a boxer a gay young boxer when me and my boxing manager pulled into town Binghampton New York for a match a six rounder or a four rounder something like that a young up and coming number my manager told people told anybodyd listen my boxer here young up and coming look Jack whens the weigh-in what times the weigh-in Jack what time five oclock Ill be back walk around town be back excuse me pardon me can you tell me wheres the bus station the train station toilets toilets for local fucking around fucking around sucking anything at all anything looks good or bad the fight itself the match is forgotten only in Waterbury Waterbury Connecticutt they wrote up this guy I was slated to meet the semi-final to something or other plastered all over the front page continued on page so and so on the sports page son of a former local champion oh would Id have loved to get him in bed eat out his asshole son of a former local champion twenty wins in a row undefeated blond rangey blue eyed just my type my type tongue literally drooling for a suck his asshole his cock couldnt barely hardly think worried about his buildup in newspapers son of a former local champion undefeated Jack I said I asked my manager how can you do this to me Jack throw me in with someone having such an awesome or what do you

70

call it reputation yes really scared thoughtless to the point where at fight time bell rang went out three punches former local champions son was down once twice bell sounded end of round one round two started as a replica only this time he was down and out and in order to revive him they had to throw water on his face blond blue eyed and actually what I wanted couldnt be expressed put into words not fight him suck him dry his asshole his cock my type rangey blond blue eyed so thats what I had to do you know before a boxing match in a town visit the bus station toilet the train station toilet action action cocks anything anybody Jack what times the weigh-in take a walk around town Jack.

Freddie Fields, author's professional boxing name

26 Joe Busa

It was a remarkable street Hanover street there was The Casino Burlesque across from Kelly & Hayes Gym one flight up where professional and amateur boxers trained downstairs a pawnshop with a trumpet clarinet and two pairs of heavily padded boxing gloves in its window hotdogs up the street next to another burlesque house Old Howard The Old Howard to be exact nearby a bookstore buying stolen books for resale Jimmy Jimmy from Washington DC keeping his habit stealing books others ordering mailorder books under fictitious names from specialty clubs speed nembutals seconals tuinals dilaudid paregoric yet to sleep with any of them any of the other drug addicts kept away scuffling if we kissed me and Joe Busa Id turn it into a squirming tease picked up by police on a really truely bum rap doing what maybe ten to fifteen so howcome howcome he isnt Joe isnt out on parole why well it was offered only Joe Joe Busas got to tell the parole board Im guilty Im guilty but hes not its a bum rap Joed come in you know Id be fixing or just finished fixing and Joed grab me hug me kiss me serious seriously and he had something Joe had something between his legs usually it was up at Yummys Yummy Taylors place the projects the red brick projects and Id be sort of embarrassed squirming out of his arms hes madly in love with me madly Im shooting up shooting up and so is he though not hardly as much anyways I dont think too late too late me Im cured Joes away Joe Busas away on a bum rap what

72

are you going to do thats it thats it hes away.

And what are you doing I asked I havent seen you in ages he was selling magazines from a bootleg stand in front of the subway stop at Union Square a far cry from Bostons Hanover street or Beacon Hill drug addicts come from Washington DC saying I squealed anyways it wasnt so so this other one he ended up doing some time on Deer Island he was from Washington DC also same as Jimmy Jimmy Waters only he wasnt stealing books.

And I was impressed impressed very much impressed with his cock he was selling shoes a lot of dope fiends sold shoes womens shoes every male dope fiend out of Washington DC it seemed to me sold womens shoes at one time or another soons you make a sale Gene told me you can draw money commission that way the other one said the one doing time on Deer Island the one that told everyone I squealed on him that way you got your money and you can leave the shoestore for a short period Ill be right back Ill be right back be back in a second so to speak and do your coping know what I mean get your stuff and shoot up in the cellar downstairs in the shoestore toilet do you understand what Im talking about you sell them everything everything not only shoes accessories pocketbooks leather gloves matching leather gloves Gene asked remember when you sucked my cock vaguely vaguely came into the store the shoestore on Tremont street rung up no sale on the register took money out of the register be right back didnt even work there didnt even work there I did though I worked there Gene said I did that yes you did that did that yes you did that repeated he said I squealed on him imagine that Gene that I squealed on him breaking into the Medford pharmacy after he finished at Deer Island he was sent to the federal can for a parole violation tattoos he had and milky white skin and a gorgeous a gorgeous cock really no kidding a gorgeous cock fat with foreskin barely covering the head a very pronounced head yet of all of them of all of those dope fiends I knew almost you can say almost intimately Joe Busa Joes the only one ever gave me a tumble know what I mean so to speak hugging me and kissing me me squirming squirming and giggling out of his arms oh Joe stop it Joe Joe youre embarrassing me Joe no I dont believe actually that they were my words.

27 Somewhere Else

F rom the courts mostly everybody has been committed for thirty day observation periods ignored by doctors until one day somebody says youre going to see the board the board a half a dozen people seated at a conference table and right away I started talking saying listen Im not sick I dont belong here you know what I thought was intelligent conversation and theyre all looking down at sheets of paper zeroxed no doubt of what I was supposed to have done to be there in the first place chased his private physician around his table no around his desk whats this physician stuff he was a doctor a psychiatrist recommended to him me by two card carrying communists gay communists it was primarily on account of I was shooting a lot of shit in those days I think breaking up with Hush and everything blaming junk everything on junk and actually loving it loving junk and this doctor this psychiatrist writing me legitimate prescriptions for dolophine and dilaudid nembutal tuinal and seconal saying Fred look Fred I dont want you buying street drugs of course by street drugs he meant horse he called it heroin and of course I complied yes as long as he kept writing legitimate prescriptions I mean what a joke who had money for horse on a steady basis hadnt I myself been forging prescriptions for the past five years forging prescriptions for the same stuff he was legitimately writing for with his valid narcotic license number stamped in the upper righthand corner of his personalized prescriptions alright so I dont know it was one thing or another pressure by people biological family city police officials so the doctor was pressured to agree for his own good and the protection of innocents including himself his patient me who chased him around his desk should be committed.

Alright so he was committed I was committed legally for observation through the law courts after a couple of weeks drinking vast quantities of instant coffee painting in oils dull palm green scenes of isolated pacific islands eating jewish food chocolate bars halvah bring me some sardines cans of sardines will you will you or else dont come to see me get me out of here get me out of here will you will you alright so after seeing the board I was attached to a special group of a dozen or so people and I think it was twice a week we were all dozen or so of us herded to the basement of the building we were housed in strapped down on individual leather covered tables told now count backwards from number twenty or thirty an hour or so later to awake upstairs lying in bed an hour or so completely obliterated.

Alright so at first I was filling his dilaudid prescriptions at the pharmacy across catty cornered across from his office the pharmacy at the intersection of Massachusetts Avenue and Beacon Street until he moved his office a short distance away to Bay State Road and he told me fill the prescriptions at The Kenmore Pharmacy located on Commonwealth Avenue in the Kenmore Square area didnt you actually catch up to the doctor punch him in the mouth bloody his mouth did I did I then then this hour or so that was occluded from my memory the technical term youve suffered occlusions maybe the ones owned the pharmacy at the intersection of Massachusetts Avenue and Beacon Street realized how valuable the prescription narcotics you know the shit dolophine dialudid nembutal tuinal and seconal were if sold so to speak under the table so alright they reneged look doctor we have nothing against you personally only how about having your patient fill his prescription somewhere else.

28 Yes Doctor Yes Doctor

There's no finer feeling than leaving a doctors office with a prescription for morphine or one of its potent derivatives going into the drugstore on Bellingham Square I'll wait for it not having to worry is the guy the pharmacist calling the croaker for verification did you write a prescription doctor thirty morphine tablets for one of the jewish kids hangs around Bellingham Square you did you didn't the police have been here doctor yes doctor yes doctor about this jewish kid forging prescriptions.

What are you what are you the cop asked you certainly don't look it I couldn't help it what was meant actually was was whose fault was it who was to blame usually don't find many jewish kids using shit do you that's a lot of crap put bluntly why is it why is it what's wrong with alcohol drinking alcohol nothing nothing nothing wrong with it hey during the second world war what was I sixteen working at the GE in Lynn city of Lynn so naive didn't even know the common rhyme don't go out the way you came in graveyard shift remember clearly like it was yesterday second world war didn't want me quitting high school get a high school education go to college learn a trade anything get out of the house pay board what five a week five dollars a week he works hard hard wash and polish his car big black Buick big black 1936 Buick 1938 Lasalle another long fat big black automobile for me to wash and polish then what a fire in the engine looking for trouble under the hood with a lighted match a wooden match lit with his thumbnail then another one a 1941 Cadillac same type of touring car shipyard carpenter anybody can hold a hammer was a certified carpenter B sticker to buy rationed gasoline what was I a young quean didn't even know it polish his automobile town actually loaded with sailors sailors and I didn't even know it heard them whole bunch of young queans public gardens going simply wild or gaga or whatever you call it something about a sailor there's something about a sailor thirteen buttons at any of two bus station toilets unhinged unbuttoned every time a sailor has to pee peering down the whole lineup through a crack in a toilet door anyway knowing enough to see what I was looking at saying to myself often oh would I love to oh would I love to.

There's no finer feeling than leaving a doctors office with a prescription for morphine or one of its potent derivatives going into the drugstore on Bellingham Square I'll wait for it not having to worry is the guy the phamacist calling the croaker for verification did you write a prescription doctor thirty morphine tablets for one of the jewish kids hangs around Bellingham Square you did you didn't the police have been here doctor yes doctor yes doctor about this jewish kid forging prescriptions.

29 Cold Shook and shot

Do you want some seafood Gamsuns thirtyfive cent luncheon special when 1938 according to the hearing test or tests seafood not for fucken thirtyfive fucken cents chow mein chop suey then later or before from eleven oclock to three oclock in the day-time after that time you pay the full price basement bargains eye ear nose and throat clinic having the same identical loss dying young overdosing on desoxin cold shook and shot.

All fingers so to speak pointed at me as we me and the others the whole shmear of tribal insanity why was he found dead dried blood mouth stained from where it gushed nothing like a good hit of speed desoxin shit put in a small bottle and shook with a syringe full of cold water else if it's hot it'll gel that's what I always said hot it'll gel he took after you he took after you shed my tears a few weeks later meanwhile I'd been upstairs not out of morbid curiosity I'd lived there myself in those two attic rooms lived there myself a few times when I'd got out of prison between bits lived there twice then when I'd get out seems like he'd be in prison so I knew the two rooms backwards and forwards so to speak pretty sure I'd find a stash hidden somewhere up there attic rooms converted into a studio refrigerator gas range toilet bath shower sinks living room bedroom in the closet in Ronald Malcom's jacket a gray suede with torn pockets I reached in felt something in the lining of the jacket tearing the pocket I was into a little wider I got out a roll of bills some two hundred odd dollars well that came in handy you know my habit and all rent of a cheap room I had in town relax a bit not having to be so tense and frantic hustling up money for the following mornings bang.

His name was Ronald Malcom Malcom was his middle name he was five years my junior had my foot in the door once once in NYC on the eastside we'd been out cashing stolen money orders that is I'd been cashing the money orders for him it was supposed to be a fifty-fifty deal fifteen thousand dollars worth a slow process going from clothing store to clothing store making a small purchase making out the money order waiting for change so anyways when I came out of a store I'd hand him the proceeds just in case something happened whatever so the money wouldn't be found on my person any ways I'd done about five thousand dollars worth when I came out of the last store he was gone money money orders originally he'd stolen them out of one of the many drugstores he'd broken into not for the money actually but for the drugs the cocaine the morphine and so forth anyways he was gone with the money we were sup-posed to split fifty-fifty also the remainder of the MO's of course I didn't care about the MO's that hadn't as yet been cashed what I was worried about first was that while I was in the last clothing store he'd somehow managed to get arrested well after a couple of hours I called the local police station nothing no he wasn't there oh oh I thought the drugs the drugs he'd been staying with me of course he had all these drugs in fact I was supposed to be selling some of the drugs for him so in turn he kept me supplied with the shit oh oh sure enough when I got back to my hotel no drugs no money no Ronald Malcom he'd left me a note and some paper you know a few uncashed money orders and here I was with an oil burner of a habit and suddenly nothing not a cent and the only way I could cash a money order or at least attempt to cash one was of course to have some drugs in my veins alright for a short time I was styimied what to do what to do how could what happened happen this this this total betrayal a betrayal that left me not only sick physically from of course the lack of proper drugs my body for so long had become accustomed to but also emotionally anyways one thing leading to another I found out where he was staying managing despite venomous denials denials that Ronald Malcom was there to get my foot wedged in the door and finally he appears threatening to stab me my foot with a knife if I don't leave and get my foot out of the door hey I think I replied I'm a dope fiend go ahead and stab away I'm not leaving until I get some money and some dope anyways he did stab my foot once once that took place though it sort of acted to stir me on hey I'm a sick dope fiend getting stabbed by a penknife in the foot by Ronald Malcom isn't going to deter me don't I know Ronald Malcom don't I know him anyways the ultimate end of the matter was I managed to bulldoze my way into this here apartment where he was staying bloody foot and all so although I forget exactly due to the traumatic effect the event had on my psyche we did arrive at a settlement him saying suddenly almost as suddenly as when he left me high and dry drugless and penniless him saying suddenly he doesn't want any trouble I don't want no trouble I don't want no trouble here's the drugs here's some money trying to make it appear I wasn't really entitled to said money and drugs until I probably told him if he didn't change his attitude I'd take all the money the drugs now it was my turn for venomous confrontations.

30 | Same Trainers

Had been to Stillman's Gym early finished training sparred a couple of rounds it's so long ago barely remember sparred a couple of rounds with either the middle-
weight or lightheavyweight contender for nothing gratis didn't
get paid because it so happened the contenders the two
contenders we had the same trainers who is he who's he the
young guy sparring met and was taken to Sardi's restaurant
by wealthy middleaged Scandinavian man had on proudly
blue french suede sports jacket later afterdinner to his room
the Scandinavians at the then prestigious Waldorf Astoria
Hotel undressed with or without vaseline oh you're a boxer
professional yes eighteen years old just turned eighteen this
past june june twentieth eighteen years old and obviously a
good fuck a pretty good fuck living steady with Hush and
getting fucked by Hush sometimes oh roughly a couple of times
a day of course the Scandinavian wasn't told thought fleeting
thought when'll be the right time to ask this guy for some
money or wait for surely surely he doesn't have to be asked so
everything sort of just slipped away a date for tomorrow
showing up the Scandinavian showing up at Stillman's Gym
next day wearing neatly expensive dark blue suit striped tie
delicate much too delicate for Stillman's Gym given the brush
off true true though had to meet Hush at Coney Island meet
him on the beach in the sand in front of the bathhouse another
close one another close call what if what if Hush ever found out

Freddie with former trainer/manager
Big Bill Wienberg

about it what happened at the bathhouse before even meeting Hush the guy with the badge saying the other guy was blowing you wasn't he in whose lockerroom booth when he saw it was the other way around thinking, oh if Hush ever finds out about this showing identification papers professional boxers license alright go ahead get out of here and don't ever come back and here's Hush there's Hush sitting with a towel on the sand where've you been where've you been no place no place Hush just got here just so happy so happy to be with Hush just like nothing ever happens yesterday today never even got any money from him the Scandinavian didn't know what it was menu written in well not understanding what even ala carte meant eighteen years old this past or that past june filet mignon coffee and a really rich piece of pastry wearing proudly blue french suede sports jacket.

31 I Mean That Was Fun

O ut busy looking for something usually junk or money for junk sometimes though even with money no junk was to be had it's a panic it's a panic had people literally sitting in gutters anything doing anything doing I mean if you had a doctor kept it quiet quiet else what I mean is people on the street other users like myself were frantic if there was just a hint a whisper hey hey did you hear so and so so and so's holding stuff why there'd be an all out rush gang looking to bang you out busy like I said looking for something I mean you could have all the money in the world so to speak what good is it without junk what good is it walking down Broadway with a hardon showing through my pants proud actually in a way that I could still raise one a hard on even during the panic why well I had my own brought it with me from New England some of it the stuff stolen from a Maine pharmacy Ronald Malcom showed me see these cans labels fifty years old laudenum that's alcohol and opium I know that I know that and the opium's all settled into a gum on the bottom and this other one see it's a bottle see you even can see it the opium well I didn't get any of that stuff maybe a little taste but the next time you go out take me with you will you maybe it was the same day I asked later in the evening about midnight it rained heavily he came by my room on Marlboro Street alright come on let's go in this rain in this downpour hurry up it was only a couple of blocks away on Commonwealth on Commonwealth Avenue so he put me in front of The Somerset Hotel the pharmacy was across the way on the first floor of this brownstone house with three bay windows Ronald Malcolm he broke the side one near the stairs yet I couldn't see a thing from where I stood in the doorway of The Somerset later he startled me I didn't even see you come out of the pharmacy he said to me I had to go to my room he lived up the street from me for a tool another screwdriver or something he went across the street back in through the same window and he came out an hour later and I didn't see a thing not a thing in fact I walked back to my room and there he was with three cardboard boxes of stuff I mean that was fun counting the different various types of narcotics we had some really really powerful stuff.

I mean it's a junk hardon it comes from sort of out of the blue it feels good though like most hardons I'd get bold with it walking down Broadway letting it stick way out acting nonchalantly matter of fact like I wasn't aware I had one a hardon an occasional guy coming the opposite way licking his lips at my hardon me reaching down giving it a little tug of course that's fun too.

86

32 Steve Poulas' Punk

There have been times when I've been literally desperate for work hard work anything where I could make a buck there were construction jobs as muckers building an underwater tunnel and you know they were making good money on that job I knew this one guy he knew I was gay he was gay himself gangster type not that I was that much different a type than he was anyway he had a muckers job in the tunnel and I said Steve how about me getting on at the tunnel how about it think you can get me a job in the tunnel I mean at one time I even belonged to the laborers union so I mean I knew the score so to speak like if Steve knew one of the foremen blah blah and so forth he says oh you're too soft for that stuff I mean like he knew I had a pretty extensive oilburner of a habit oh Freddie ha ha he laughed at me you could never do the work of course I knew better that it wasn't true long's I had some junk in me three or four hundred dollars a week these muckers were bringing home of course at this time I did have my little short change hype for fifty sixty dollars a day but you knw there's nothing more secure than a steady weeks pay at least that's what I told myself but what really really upset me is when Steve said your too soft too soft for the job Freddie not that it couldn't have been a true fact only it was then that I realized how some people looked at me me I mean I was once an athlete and I mean I used to jog a couple of miles a day oh that Steve he's another story entirely later on a few years later when I got sent to prison I happened to get hold of a Boston newspaper and there's a picture on the front page of Steve Poulas bartender manager of Cavana's Bar & Grill sprawled on the sidewalk in front of Cavana's with a couple of bullets in the stomach and I found out later when I got out that it was his ex-boy friend that shot him and there was a whole mish-mash of a sexual scandal involved where Steve was madly in love still and forcing himself on his ex so the ex just waited one night until Steve got done work and let him have it and the funny thing about it is the ex-boy friend could have got out of going to prison if he'd agree in court not to testify about how they had sex and everything in detail I mean it was Steve's family that I understood wanted it covered up a moneyed greek family I believe but this jerky boy friend wanted to boast about how he's so to speak killed the monster Steve Poulas claiming he himself the ex was really not gay at all but straight and that Steve used to arrange to watch him have sex with females I mean what a crock of shit that was so anyways the courts sent him up for fifteen or twenty years and who cares not me no but actually the real story was that Steve Poulas was married with three or four young children and the boy friend would supposedly have sex with his wife while Steve watched so that's what they Steve's immediate family wanted covered up in court and so the boy friend could have got off with maybe a probation if he kept his mouth shut but obviously he didn't and they sent him up.